What teachers
need to know about
Reading and writing
difficulties

D1520718

What teachers
need to know about
Reading and writing
difficulties

PETER WESTWOOD

ACER Press

First published 2008
by ACER Press, an imprint of
Australian Council for Educational Research Ltd
19 Prospect Hill Road, Camberwell
Victoria, 3124, Australia

www.acerpress.com.au
sales@acer.edu.au

Edited by Carolyn Glascodine
Cover and text design by Mary Mason
Typeset by Mary Mason
Printed in Australia by Ligare

National Library of Australia Cataloguing-in-Publication data:

Author: Westwood, Peter S. (Peter Stuart), 1936–
Title: What teachers need to know about reading and writing difficulties /
           Peter Westwood.
ISBN: 9780864319609 (pbk.)
Series: What teachers need to know about
Notes: Includes index.
           Bibliography.
Subjects: Learning disabilities.
           Reading disabilities.
           Literacy.
Dewey Number: 371.9

Contents

Preface

The ability to read and write is fundamental to all areas of learning in the school curriculum. Literacy skills determine not only school success but also influence an individual's chances of finding and retaining satisfying work beyond school, achieving financial stability, maintaining personal autonomy and promoting self-esteem (American Federation of Teachers, 2007; OECD, 2008). It is not surprising therefore that alarm has been expressed in recent years concerning the number of students who, for a variety of reasons, fail to acquire adequate facility with reading and writing.

This book explores some of the causes of literacy problems and provides practical advice on methods that can support students with these difficulties. Many additional online resources are also identified.

As with other titles in the *What teachers need to know* series, I have drawn extensively on research and professional literature from many countries, particularly the United Kingdom, the United States of America and Australia. Problems in literacy are of international concern. I hope that the extensive reference list will be of value to teachers and others who may wish to pursue some issues in greater depth.

The topic of spelling has been covered only briefly in this volume because a separate monograph (*What teachers need to know about spelling*) deals with the topic in much greater detail.

My sincere thanks to Carolyn Glascodine for carrying out the editorial work on the original manuscript. Thanks also to the staff at ACER for their support.

PETER WESTWOOD

RESOURCES www.acer.edu.au/need2know

Readers may access the online resources mentioned
throughout this book through direct links at
www.acer.edu.au/need2know

one

Current issues in literacy learning and teaching

KEY ISSUES

- **Learning difficulties in literacy:** It is surprising – given what we know about effective methods for teaching reading and writing – that so many students slip through the net and do not achieve full literacy.
- **Causes:** There are many possible causes of difficulty in learning to read and write, some environmental and some intrinsic to the learner.
- **Methods:** The current perspective is that teaching methods should combine the motivational and contextual principles of the whole language approach with the proven benefits of explicit teaching of essential decoding skills and comprehension strategies.
- **Preventing literacy problems:** Prevention requires an understanding of the causes of such problems, and knowledge of effective methods of instruction.
- **Teacher training:** Prevention of literacy problems requires well-trained teachers who can implement effective methods with high fidelity.

The cornerstone of academic achievement and the foundation for success across the curriculum is learning to read and write proficiently (Wilson & Trainin, 2007, p. 257).

Few would disagree that one of the most important goals of education has always been that all students should learn to read and write with adequate proficiency. It is surprising therefore – given the information, skills and resources available to schools today – that a significant number of our students do not achieve this basic goal. Their failure to cope with the demands of reading and writing has an extremely detrimental effect on their self-esteem, confidence, attitude, motivation, and their ability to learn across the curriculum. Rose (2006) has observed that without the ability to communicate and learn effectively through reading and writing, individuals are severely disadvantaged for life. Similarly, Moats (1999, p. 5) remarks that:

> Reading is the fundamental skill upon which all formal education depends. Research now shows that a child who doesn't learn the reading basics early is unlikely to learn them at all. Any child who doesn't learn to read early and well will not easily master other skills and knowledge, and is unlikely to ever flourish in school or in life.

The OECD (2008) confirms that an individual's literacy standard is related to his or her quality of life, employability and earning capacity. Schools have a duty therefore to ensure that standards are high, and that the most effective teaching methods and materials are used. Hempenstall (2005) suggests that in Australian schools between 20 and 40 per cent of students do not make optimum progress in learning to read, and he comments: 'There is increasing consensus that if the best available practice were being emphasised in our school system, reading problems could be reduced to less than 10%; indeed, some say 5%' (p. 14).

Prevalence of literacy learning difficulties

Although some authorities dispute the notion that there is a serious problem with literacy standards (e.g., McQuillan, 1998; Sawyer & Watson, 1997), there is ample evidence to the contrary. According to an OECD (2008) report, almost one-third of students in countries like the United Kingdom, the United States of America, France and Germany have significant difficulty when it comes to everyday reading tasks such as understanding a bus timetable or comprehending directions on a food packet or medicine label. The Australian Bureau of Statistics (ABS, 2007) provides data revealing that in 2006, approximately 46 per cent of the population had some difficulties with 'prose reading' (narrative texts, newspapers, brochures) and 47 per cent had difficulties with 'document reading' (forms, schedules, tables). These figures represent approximately 7 million Australians who experience problems with everyday literacy. Of these weak readers, approximately 18 per cent perform at an extremely low level of competence (ABS, 2007). Similar statistics from countries such as the United Kingdom and the United States of America suggest that at least 30 to 35 per cent of school students have difficulties with reading and writing (Blanton et al., 2007; Exley, 2007; National Council on Teacher Quality, 2006). It is also reported that a large number of students drop out of high school, in large part because they lack the literacy skills to cope with the secondary school curriculum (American Federation of Teachers, 2007).

The proportion of individuals with literacy problems seems to increase as students get older. In disadvantaged secondary schools in the United Kingdom for example, it is reported that the number of students with reading comprehension difficulties can be as high as 58 per cent (Myers & Botting, 2008). In secondary schools in the United States of America, some 70 per cent of older readers require some form of remediation or additional support when dealing with expository texts (Biancrosa & Snow, 2006). In addition, universities and colleges report that many undergraduates have difficulties coping with the literacy demands of their courses (e.g., Lietz, 1996; Perin, 2006).

The Australian *National School English Literacy Survey* (Masters & Forster, 1997a) found that 27 per cent of students in Year 3, and 29 per cent of students in Year 5, did not reach the required standard in writing, spelling and reading – with male students, ESL students, students from lower socio-economic backgrounds, and Indigenous students over-represented in the lowest achievement group. In Australia as a whole, students in the top 10 per cent of reading achievement in Years 3 and 5 are working about *5 years ahead* of the weakest 10 per cent (Masters & Forster, 1997b).

Some indication of the number of students with the most severe literacy difficulties can be seen in data from the regular Australian literacy benchmark assessments. The testing in 2006 revealed that some 12 per cent of students in Year 5, and 13 per cent in Year 7, failed to achieve even the minimum standard required in reading (MCEETYA, 2008). This situation has not changed much in over a decade since the benchmark assessments were first introduced, despite a high level of public concern and much activity and intervention on the part of policy makers between 1996 and 2008.

The departments of education in all states and territories in Australia have acknowledged that a problem exists and have included priorities for early identification and intervention within their literacy action plans. For example, the South Australian Government confirms that while many students achieve at a high standard, too many at-risk students consistently perform below acceptable levels in literacy and numeracy. The challenge is to close this achievement gap (South Australian Government, 2007).

Potential causes of literacy learning problems

There are, of course, many possible reasons why a student may experience difficulty learning to read, write and spell in the early years of schooling. Some of the problems may be due to factors intrinsic to the student, while others are due to outside influences. Of the outside influences, teaching method is one of the most powerful.

> *Teaching method*

Many years ago, Alm (1981) pointed out that ineffective educational practices (i.e. teaching methods) contribute to children's difficulty in learning to read and write. More recently, teaching approach as a major causal factor has been strongly confirmed. Several national reports conclude that certain teaching methods are far more effective than others in teaching children to read (e.g., DEST, 2005; House of Commons Education and Skills Committee, UK, 2005; National Reading Panel, US, 2000; Rose, 2006). But these reports also note that these effective methods are not always used in our schools.

Research studies indicate clearly that children need to be taught explicitly the principles for applying phonic knowledge (letter-to-sound correspondences) in order to decode and spell unfamiliar words (for reviews, see Adams, 1990; Coltheart & Prior, 2006; de Lemos, 2005; Tan et al., 2007). According to Simmons et al. (2007), there is a window of opportunity to teach young children these decoding skills, using well-focused and intensive instruction. Finn (2000, p. iii) suggests that, 'Millions of children are needlessly classified as 'disabled' when, in fact, their main problem is that nobody taught them to read when they were five and six years old'.

> Time allocated for learning

The amount of time devoted to instruction and practice in reading and writing is an important influence on literacy development (Biancrosa & Snow, 2006; Kourea et al., 2007). In busy primary classrooms it is easy for time allocated to literacy to be eroded by other pressures. Insufficient practice time impacts most severely on the least able readers and writers. In the United Kingdom, the daily 'literacy hour' was introduced to ensure that in every primary classroom at least that amount of time is spent in focused literacy activities. The literacy hour has also been implemented in many Australian schools.

> Language ability

Other outside influences on reading and writing include the language environment of the home in which young children spend their early formative years. The language development of some children is not stimulated adequately in some environments, and children may come to school lacking the vocabulary and syntactical knowledge necessary for understanding a teacher's 'language of instruction' and for processing the language of books. It is known that language ability, particularly vocabulary knowledge, is one of the strongest predictors of successful entry into reading (Hay & Fielding-Barnsley, 2006; Myers & Botting, 2008; Wise et al., 2007a). Inadequate exposure to talk, books and print during the preschool years not only restricts children's language and literacy awareness, it does not prepare them adequately for learning to read when they begin school. Meiers et al. (2006) report that in Australia there are wide variations in children's abilities and readiness to learn when they first enter school, and the impact of these differences are evident throughout the first three years of schooling.

> *Phonological awareness*

Children with underdeveloped language skills (and many other students too) may also have greater difficulty developing phonemic awareness – that is, sensitivity to the speech sounds contained within words. An understanding that spoken words can be reduced to a sequence of separate sounds is essential for grasping the principle of the alphabetic code we use for writing in English (Adams, 1990; Ehri et al., 2001b; McCardle et al., 2002). Learning and using phonic skills (the ability to associate letters with sounds for decoding words in print) relies entirely upon good phonemic awareness – and good teaching (Eldredge, 2005). It is reported that well over one-third of beginning readers have a poor level of phonemic awareness (National Council on Teacher Quality, 2006); and there is abundant evidence to show that lack of phonemic awareness is a major cause of learning difficulties in reading and spelling (e.g., Adams, 1990; Silva & Alves-Martins, 2003; Wise et al., 2007b). More will be said in Chapter 2 on the importance of developing phonemic awareness.

> *Social or cultural disadvantage*

In terms of other environmental influences on literacy learning, there is evidence that certain groups are over-represented among the population of students with literacy difficulties – for example, ESL students, students from lower socio-economic backgrounds and Indigenous students (Commonwealth Department of Education, Science and Training, 2002; MCEETYA, 2008; Masters & Forster, 1997a; 1997b). Social, cultural and linguistic factors interact for these particular groups, predisposing some students to educational risk. Opportunities to learn may be diminished through frequent absences from school, low expectations of success and literacy not being highly valued. For such children, learning to read and write effectively may represent such an uphill battle that they opt out of the race. In doing so, the achievement gap widens between those with good literacy skills and those without (Teale et al., 2008).

> *Factors intrinsic to the learner*

Intrinsic factors that may inhibit literacy learning in individual students include weak cognitive ability (general intelligence), deficiencies in relevant psychological processes (such as working memory and visual or auditory perception) and attitudinal and behavioural aspects (such as motivation, concentration span and attention to task). Ways in which these processes are involved in reading, both at word recognition level and when comprehending text will be discussed in more detail later. A few students have a particular constellation of such difficulties that comprise what has become known as a *specific learning disability* (SpLD) – *dyslexia* in the case of reading, and *dysgraphia* in the case of writing. In SpLD, the core deficit appears to be a major problem with phonological awareness, often coupled with an inability to retrieve information such as words or letter-to-sound relationships rapidly from memory (Escribano, 2007; Wolf & Bowers, 1999). These students are often most accurately identified by their very slow (sometimes negligible) response to intensive remedial intervention.

> *Affective response to failure*
Finally, learning difficulties in literacy are seriously compounded by the detrimental emotional effects of failure that are experienced by most students with these problems (Blanton et al., 2007; Westwood, 2004). Persistent lack of success causes frustration, loss of motivation and diminished self-esteem. This in turn causes the student to disengage further from learning and to be resistant to help. Wilson and Trainin (2007) confirm that early perceptions of ability or lack of ability influence students' future levels of engagement and success.

The need for a balanced approach to instruction

The teaching of reading has undergone many changes over the years, from the alphabet (letter names) method of the late 1800s, through various waves of phonics instruction (letter–sound correspondences), to look-and-say (whole word recognition), and more recently to the whole language approach that stresses reading for meaning rather than decoding.[1] Currently, whole language is losing ground in most countries because, as stated above,

---

1 For an excellent online history of the teaching of reading see Wilson (2003) at: http://www.zona-pellucida.com/wilson10.html

research evidence suggests that beginning readers require explicit and direct teaching of phonic decoding skills if they are to become confident independent readers (Raven, 2003; Wheldall, 2006).

Whole language, as usually implemented, contains too little systematic instruction in phonics and relies too much on incidental or 'natural' learning. Studies by Berninger et al. (2003) at second-grade level have confirmed that explicit instruction in word recognition, combined with explicit instruction in comprehension strategies produces the best results, particularly with low-achieving students. At an even earlier stage of learning, Xue and Meisels (2004) report that a combination of phonics instruction and what they termed 'integrated language arts' (whole language by another name) produces a better result than either method used alone. This large-scale study at kindergarten level gave support to the view that phonics instruction is even more effective when combined with an integrated literacy approach.

It is interesting to note that in the United States of America, two key associations that have tended to be strongly child-centred and whole language in their philosophies – the International Reading Association and the National Association for the Education of Young Children – issued a joint statement in 1998, pointing out to members that the ability to read and write does not develop naturally and requires careful planning and instruction. They also confirmed that the teaching program should contain systematic instruction in decoding, along with meaningful connected reading (IRA/NAEYC, 1998).

The approach now strongly recommended is a balanced approach that retains the motivating and authentic elements of whole language while at the same time ensuring that decoding skills and comprehension strategies are directly taught and thoroughly practised (Ellis, 2005; Hall & Harding, 2003; Pressley, 2006; Tompkins, 2006). To clarify this further, Raven (2003) states that a balanced literacy approach retains the use of good literature to be read to and by children, creative writing, independent reading, teacher-guided reading, the use of graded books (vocabulary controlled and decodable), plus explicit, systematic phonics instruction. Similarly, Pikulski (1997) makes a case that effective reading programs must have a balance between explicit teaching of skills and strategies, and using those skills and strategies to read and respond to a wide variety of texts.

Such advice is immanently sensible, but it has become popular in some quarters to criticise the notion of a 'balanced' program, implying instead that the approach to beginning reading must be *entirely* focused on phonics instruction (Hempenstall, 2006; Moats, 2000; Moats, 2007; Stern, 2005; Wren, n.d., Welna, 1999). The criticism seems to be that whole language advocates have simply highjacked the term 'balanced approach' and used it to rename whole language without any serious attempt to embed more systematic phonics instruction. Stern (2005, n.p.) comments, 'Balanced literacy is the brand name for an instructional approach that adds a dollop of phonics to an otherwise whole language reading program in which children are encouraged to construct or decipher meaning from so-called authentic texts'. And in her paper titled *Whole language lives on: The illusion of 'balanced' reading instruction*, Moats (2000) does not believe it is even feasible to fuse systematic instruction with whole language practices. This view is extreme; and it could be argued with equal force that in practical terms it is absolutely impossible to operate a meaningful literacy program that is *entirely* focused on phonics instruction.

There is much evidence that a balanced approach in beginning reading can be achieved. For example, Donat (2006) describes *Reading their Way*, a grade K–1 program, and claims that it is perfectly feasible to combine phonics instruction with whole language to increase beginning readers' achievements. *Reading their Way* integrates phoneme awareness training and phonics with contextual instruction in reading, writing and spelling. To some extent, the *Four Blocks Literacy Model* (Cunningham et al., 2001) also represents a balanced approach, with due attention given to guided reading, self-selected book reading, writing and working with words (in which phonics and spelling are explicitly taught). Willows (2002) is even more specific, and suggests that a truly balanced literacy program gives attention to each of the following components:

▶ motivation
▶ language development
▶ listening and thinking
▶ concepts about print
▶ word knowledge
▶ sight vocabulary

- phonemic awareness
- letter–sound correspondences
- reading fluency
- comprehension strategies
- exposure to a variety of texts
- handwriting
- spelling
- writing conventions
- composing strategies
- grammar and syntax.

The notion of balance can go beyond the actual content of the literacy program. Topping and Ferguson (2005) suggest that balance is also needed between whole-class, small-group and individual teaching patterns, and between teacher direction (demonstrating, modelling, explaining, questioning) and student-centred independent activity and practice. Balance is also required in addressing what Freebody (1992) refers to as the 'four roles of the effective reader', namely *code breaker* (using a knowledge of phonics, contextual cues, grammar and text structure), *text participant* (making meaning, relating information to prior knowledge and experience), *text user* (applying reading skills for authentic purposes), and *text analyst* (understanding text structure, functions and purpose). Balance here implies that none of the roles are overlooked or overemphasised.

Teacher effectiveness and teacher preparation

Several writers have suggested that the quality of a teacher is more important than any particular method or model of instruction in ensuring that students develop essential literacy skills (Topping & Ferguson, 2005; Wilson, 2003). Certain teachers appear to produce positive learning outcomes for even the most difficult students by using a variety of approaches and making modifications to the balance between skills and application.

In recent years there has been a focus in classroom research on what it is that effective teachers of literacy actually do that makes a difference in students' learning (Flynn, 2007; Hall & Harding, 2003; Louden et al., 2005; Ministry of Education, NZ, 2007; Topping & Ferguson, 2005; Tse et al., 2007). Taking the study by Louden et al. (2005) as an example, the researchers investigated six key dimensions of teachers' classroom practices and concluded (p. 242) that:

> Considered together, the findings of this study have led us to conclude that effective early literacy teaching requires teachers who can ensure high levels of student participation, are deeply knowledgeable about literacy learning, can simultaneously orchestrate a variety of classroom activities, can support and scaffold learning at word and text levels, can target and differentiate their instruction and can do all this in classrooms characterised by mutual respect [between students and teacher].

A key point in the quotation above is that teachers need to be 'deeply know-ledgeable about literacy learning'. A current burning issue is the question of whether teachers-in-training are receiving adequate and appropriate instruction in a wide range of methods and materials for teaching literacy skills to a diverse population of learners (Coltheart & Prior, 2006; de Lemos, 2005; National Council on Teacher Quality, 2006; Spear-Swerling, 2007). Even the joint statement from International Reading Association and National Association for the Education of Young Children (IR A/ NAEYC, 1998) acknowledges that teachers are inadequately prepared to teach reading, and calls for improved pre- and in-service training.

Coltheart and Prior (2006) cite evidence to show that in most teacher education courses in Australia, less than 10 per cent of the available time is devoted to preparing student teachers to teach reading; and in about half the courses the time allocated is *less than 5 per cent*. These writers also note that many beginning teachers' own literacy skills are not strong, and they have little real understanding of many of the concepts underpinning children's literacy learning. They comment that, 'New teachers are graduating without sufficient specific strategies to improve literacy standards' (Coltheart & Prior, 2006, p. 161), and they recommend that, 'Teacher education and training should include more specific and evidence-based training in the teaching of reading and include ongoing professional learning throughout the teaching career' (p. 161). On similar ground, De Lemos (2005) observes that there appears to be a discrepancy between the practices that research has found to be most effective and the practices that are taught in pre-service teacher education courses. The report titled *Quality of School Education* prepared by the Senate Standing Committee on Employment, Workplace Relations and Education (2007) highlights some of the current shortcomings in the professional preparation of Australian teachers for the teaching of literacy (see the Links box at the end of the chapter).

These issues of inadequate training are not unique to Australia. In the United States of America it is said that the extensive knowledge required to teach reading and spelling is underestimated by staff in most university departments of education, and too little coverage is given to it (Moats, 1999; Spear-Swerling, 2007). There appears to be a very large gap between what research has revealed about learning to read and what beginning teachers are taught to believe. In the publication titled *What education schools aren't teaching about reading and what elementary teachers aren't learning*, the National Council on Teacher Quality (NCTQ) (2006) reports that only 15 per cent of 72 schools of education in United States of America are providing student teachers with even minimal exposure to *research* information on reading (i.e., the 'science' of reading); and phonics instruction is not taught in six out of seven teacher education courses. Instead, these courses are espousing holistic and unstructured methods that have been largely discredited and that do not meet the needs of up to 40 per cent of school population. As a result, beginning teachers lack any depth of knowledge about phonics, word recognition, comprehension, and spelling strategies – and are therefore unlikely to give good instruction in these areas. NCTQ (2006, p. 27) makes the telling observation: 'Our findings were somewhat surprising, suggesting that some college professors may not be teaching the science of reading because they are ideologically opposed to the science but because they may be reluctant to teach what they themselves do not know'. The situation is probably very similar in Australia at this time.

The number of students experiencing learning difficulties in reading and writing is unlikely to decrease until teachers are in a position to implement truly effective, evidence-based methods. These methods will be discussed in the following chapters.

LINKS TO MORE ON CURRENT ISSUES

▶ National benchmark data for students in Years 3, 5 and 7 in Australian schools is available online at: http://www.mceetya.edu.au/mceetya/anr/

▶ An excellent paper, *Preventing early reading failure* (Torgesen, 2004) discusses some of the causes of reading difficulty and highlights appropriate interventions to overcome these. Available online at: http://www.aft.org/pubs-reports/american_educator/issues/fall04/reading.htm

▶ The Executive Summary from the report of the US Committee on the Prevention of Reading Difficulties in Young Children (National Research Council, 1998) contains very important recommendations on teaching methods. Available online at: http://www.nap.edu/readingroom/books/reading/

▶ National Council on Teacher Quality. (2006). *A study of what is and is not being taught to pre-service teachers in US university schools of education.* Available online at: http://www.nctq.org/nctq/images/nctq_reading_study_app.pdf

▶ Moats, L. (1999). *Reading IS rocket science: What expert teachers of reading should know and be able to do.* Washington, DC: American Federation of Teachers. An important and influential document indicating what teachers should know about the nuts and bolts of teaching reading (and how most teacher education courses fall short in providing this coverage). Available online at: http://www.aft.org/pubs-reports/downloads/teachers/rocketsci.pdf

▶ The report of the *In Teachers' Hands Project* (Louden et al. 2005) and the monograph that summarises the findings can be located online at: http://inteachershands.education.ecu.edu.au/

▶ The Senate Standing Committee Report *Quality of school education* (2007) is available online at: http://www.aph.gov.au/Senate/committee/eet_ctte/academic_standards/report/report.pdf

Reading difficulties at word level

- **The simple view of reading:** Reading involves two main processes – identifying words and comprehending connected text.
- **How do readers identify words?** The answer to this question has implications for teaching.
- **Phonological and phonic skills:** Taken together, these skills provide the foundation for word identification. They need to be taught early, and by direct methods.
- **Sight vocabulary:** It is essential that students build a memory store of words they can recognise instantly without the need for decoding.

Proficiency in reading basically involves gaining competence in two separate but complementary processes, namely word identification (decoding) and linguistic comprehension. To become competent readers, students need to learn effective strategies for identifying all words in print and for comprehending text. Literacy instruction must therefore include explicit teaching and practice in these essential strategies to enable all students to read fluently, confidently and with understanding (Pressley, 2006).

This chapter provides information on common difficulties with word identification and decoding, and offers some suggestions for instruction. Reading comprehension is covered fully in the chapter that follows.

The simple view of reading

The notion that just two processes can account for reading ability underpins what is known as 'the simple view of reading' (Hoover & Gough, 1990; Gough & Tunmer, 1986; Myers & Botting, 2008; Tan et al., 2007). This view is certainly simple when compared to the multi-faceted and highly esoteric view of reading that has emerged from the field of so-called 'New Literacy Studies' (NLS) (e.g., Brandt & Clinton, 2002; Gee, 1996; Luke & Carrington, 2002). NLS adopts a cultural and sociolinguistic perspective on literacy acquisition, rather than a cognitive-psychological perspective. While the social and cultural view may help teachers appreciate how learners' environmental background, beliefs, expectations and value systems impact upon literacy practices and motivation, the cognitive perspective has more immediate and useful implications for teaching and intervention.

The 'simple view of reading' can be readily accepted as a viable starting point for discussion because it has obvious practical implications. Wren (2003) describes the model as 'powerful' in that it has predictive validity – for example, decoding and comprehension skills both predict reading achievement fairly accurately – and it has great practical value because it highlights the two key processes on which to focus explicit instruction and guided practice. Tan et al. (2007) attest to the value of this model for identifying instructional priorities when working with low-progress readers in remedial contexts.

In the United Kingdom, the simple view of reading has been adopted in the National Literacy Strategy to provide the framework for teaching reading in primary schools. In the United Kingdom it is stated that:

> Learning to read … involves setting up processes by which the words on the page can be recognised and understood, and continuing to develop the language processes that underlie both spoken and written language comprehension. Both sets of processes are necessary for reading; but neither is sufficient on its own (DCSF, 2006, p. 2).

How do we identify words in print?

Burns et al. (1999, p. 88) state that:

> For a child to read fluently, he or she must recognize words at a glance, and use the conventions of letter–sound correspondences automatically. Without these word recognition skills, children will never be able to read or understand text comfortably and competently.

A key issue for teachers to consider is what strategies do competent readers use to identify words? If we know how words are recognised, we can use this information to guide instruction.

Words are actually identified in several different ways, some requiring greater cognitive effort than others on the part of the reader, and some requiring a greater degree of linguistic competence. Some strategies are immediately available, even to beginning readers, but others only develop after considerable experience and extensive practice in reading connected text. Word identification strategies are not mutually exclusive, and two or more are often used together in an integrated way. The most common methods for identifying a word include the following.

> *Automatic recall*
This involves retrieving the word instantly and automatically from memory. We say that the word is contained within the reader's *sight vocabulary*.

> *Using phonic knowledge*
The letters in the word are associated with their equivalent phonemes and these sounds are blended to produce the word. Words that are frequently encountered and decoded in this way ultimately become part of sight vocabulary and do not need to be decoded again.

> *Using orthographic units within the word*
Orthographic units are groups of letters that, taken together, suggest a probable pronunciation for part of the word. Recognition of this cluster of letters is sufficient to trigger immediate recognition of the whole word. Small words, such as 'it', 'she' and 'was' are complete orthographic units in themselves, and easily recognised. In more complex words such as 'computer' the

orthographic units of value for reading may be 'com' or 'comp', 'pute' or 'ute' and 'er'. The ability to perceive orthographic units automatically only comes after extensive reading experience that has exposed a reader many times to these commonly occurring letter patterns. You are almost certainly using orthographic word identification skills with a high degree of automaticity as you read this page. You are not sounding out the letters of each word, nor are you using whole-word recognition other than for the very small, high-frequency words. You are attending sufficiently – but subconsciously – to specific groups of letters that, supported by meaning and your own linguistic awareness, results in immediate word identification. Knowledge of orthographic units allows you, for example, to read the following nonsense words without needing to engage in letter-by-letter decoding: TRUP PREDDING DASTROLLIC. It is familiarity with groups of letters that make up pronounceable units that underpins swift and proficient reading (De Jong & Share, 2007). Scientific studies of the eye movements of individuals while reading confirm that individuals do process print in this way, fixating momentarily on orthographic units (Rayner, 1997).

> Using analogy

This involves mentally comparing the unfamiliar word, or parts of the word, with a known word (e.g. *east* will help with reading *eastern*, *easterly*, or *yeast*).

> Using the context of the sentence or paragraph

This is predicting a word from the meaning of a sentence. This is the least reliable strategy for word identification, but using context is a valuable back-up or confirmation after a word has been processed by any of the routes listed above. Children should not be encouraged simply to guess words they do not recognise. This is one issue on which there is major disagreement between whole language advocates and those who support a phonic approach.

Word identification problems

Proficient and experienced readers draw flexibly on any or several of the five word identification methods as appropriate; but beginning readers and students with learning difficulties have a more limited range of options available. For example, beginning readers have had too little opportunity to establish an extensive sight vocabulary, so their ability to recognise words instantly is restricted. They are more dependent on guessing words and on using cues from pictures that may accompany the text. The only reliable way that beginning readers can begin to identify new words is to acquire useful phonic knowledge to help them decode a word letter by letter. This is why systematic instruction in phonic skills is required very early in a child's journey toward literacy, and why mastery of phonics should not be left to incidental learning.

Weak readers at any age are not skilled at rapid word recognition. In particular, they have problems identifying words with irregular spelling patterns (Ricketts et al., 2008). This is due in part to their lack of reading experience and practice, and in part to lack of effective decoding strategies. Like beginners, they usually have to resort to guessing the word from context – but guessing is extremely unreliable. They may try letter-by-letter phonic decoding, but often their phonic skills, particularly sound blending, are inadequate. This makes the decoding process slow and inaccurate, overloading their working memory and impairing comprehension (Gunning, 2000; Jenkins & O'Connor, 2001). Chan and Dally, (2000, p. 165) clearly describe the basic problems thus:

> Whereas good readers become fast and accurate at recognising words without context and within context, poor readers often remain dependent on context. The use of context to identify unfamiliar words and the labour-intensive efforts of poor readers to decode words, due to deficits in either phonological or orthographic processing, tax the limited resources of working memory. When the lower-level skills of word recognition are not automatic less attention is available for comprehending the meaning of text. The problems of lack of reading fluency (demands on working memory to hold words of a sentence long enough to derive its meaning) and effortful recognition of unfamiliar words compromise higher order processes such as comprehension and learning from texts.

One obvious goal for instruction with these students is to increase, by any means possible, their acquisition of sight vocabulary. In particular, these students should master the recognition of a core of the most commonly occurring, everyday words, and should be able to read these words in context and out of context with a high degree of automaticity. Even more important, these students need to be taught to apply effective phonic skills. To help build students' confidence and competence in applying phonics in the early stages, it is often beneficial to use books that have been deliberately written to contain a high percentage of regular and decodable words. It is unfortunate that in many schools books of this type were abandoned with the advent of whole language.

Phonological skills

For some students, prior to instruction in phonics, it is necessary to concentrate first on ensuring that they have developed sufficient phonological awareness to attend to sounds within words and to appreciate the underlying concept of using letters to represent those sounds. Wise et al. (2007a, p. 1094) observe that, 'Once children begin to recognise the phonemic elements of spoken words they can then begin to establish grapheme-phoneme correspondences that provide the basis for word identification skills'.

As indicated briefly in Chapter 1, it is believed that very many students with reading and spelling difficulties have a poor phonological awareness (Ehri et al., 2001b; McCardle et al., 2002; Wise et al., 2007b). Without this awareness it is almost impossible for a learner to grasp the principle underpinning the alphabetic code, and thus master the phonic decoding skills necessary for identifying unfamiliar words and for spelling. Fortunately, there is abundant evidence available to support the notion that providing specific training in listening for sounds within words has a beneficial impact on reading and spelling for young children and for other students with learning difficulties (Donnell, 2007; Ehri et al., 2001b; Ehri, et al., 2007; Jenkins & O'Connor, 2001; Nicholson, 2006). It should be noted however that a just few students with phonemic awareness problems seem to be fairly resistant to phonological training and require much longer to acquire the necessary skills (Whiteley et al., 2007).

The most effective early intervention programs for literacy are constructed on a firm foundation of phonological training activities linked closely with explicit instruction in letter-to-sound correspondences (Donnell, 2007; Hurry & Sylva, 2007; Whiteley et al., 2007; Wise et al., 2007b). It is clear that such training is essential for beginning readers and for any student who is having significant difficulties in word identification. Suggestions for developing phonological awareness and phonic skills are presented later.

While phonological weaknesses are regarded as the core deficit in most cases of severe reading difficulty, it is evident that not *every* student with a reading and spelling problem has these difficulties (Johnston & Morrison, 2007). Other factors beyond phonological awareness are also implicated in severe reading failure (Savage & Frederickson, 2006). Such factors include limited vocabulary knowledge, deficits in working memory, and problems with rapid retrieval of letter–sound correspondences and words from memory. In cases of the most severe reading difficulty (dyslexia) the students may have the double deficit of both phonological problems and difficulties in rapid retrieval of orthographic information from memory (Vukovic & Siegel, 2006; Wolf & Bowers, 1999).

The situation with students who simply can't quickly retrieve a word that they have already stored in memory (the 'tip-of-the tongue' phenomenon, or simply very slow processing) presents a challenging case for teachers. Inability to recall such information rapidly is actually recognised as a specific learning disability and is termed *dysnomia*. In literacy research it has been named the *word finding difficulty* (WFD). Ehri and Rosenthal (2007) and Aaron et al. (1999) report that memory for words is closely associated with the meaning, pronunciation and spelling of the word, and all three should be stressed to aid memorisation and recall. Interestingly, German and Newman (2007) have found that children with a word finding difficulty can comprehend text much better when reading silently than when reading aloud, presumably because too much cognitive effort goes into the retrieval process involved in pronouncing the words aloud.

Developing phonological awareness

As stated above, phonological awareness underpins the understanding of the alphabetic code and facilitates the learning of phonic decoding skills (Ehri et al., 2001b). Students with weak phonological skills and limited phonic knowledge have great difficulty achieving swift and easy word recognition.

Children who are developing normally and who have been exposed to appropriate language stimulation in the home environment easily develop awareness that spoken words are made up from separate sounds. Stories, rhymes and songs used with preschool children can all pave the way to heightening awareness that some words share common initial sounds, some words rhyme, some words seem to comprise two or more words (e.g. *break-fast, under-ground, super-market*) and so forth. In other words, normal language experience provides the foundation not only for vocabulary development but also for tuning children's listening attention to the phonological properties of spoken words. However, it is estimated that over one-third of children entering school lack phonemic awareness and therefore require specific training in this skill if they are not to be placed at risk of developing difficulties in reading and spelling (National Council on Teacher Quality, 2006).

Consensus from research studies suggests that phonological training is most effective when it also incorporates the beginnings of phonics instruction (Lovett et al., 2000). Teaching letter–sound relationships helps focus children's listening attention on speech sounds. In addition, the use of invented spelling by children in the early stages of writing almost certainly helps strengthen phonemic awareness and phonic knowledge by causing children to think of sounds within words. Often, of course, a child's invented spelling will be inaccurate because it is not always easy to work out the exact letters needed to spell a particular word.

The aspects of phonology that are usually addressed in pre- and early-phonics training programs include:

> *Rhyming*
Rhyming involves listening to and repeating rhymes; finding words that rhyme; generating a new word to rhyme with a given word. Understanding the concept of rhyme makes it easier later for a child to recognise and use the letter groups that represent those rhymes (for example, the orthographic unit /and/ in *band, hand, sand, land*. 'Word families' are often constructed based on letter groups representing the rhyming units. Attention to rhyme and the use of word families can be incorporated in all beginning reading approaches.

> *Alliteration*
'Tall Tom takes two tomatoes'; 'Some snakes slide silently sideways'. These examples, and others, help the child to attend fully to beginning sounds – an important starting point in phonics instruction.

> *Blending*

This is the ability to combine a sequence of sounds into syllables, and syllables into words. Listening games such as 'I spy' are helpful here: 'I spy with my little eye a picture of a *fr – o – g*'. Sound blending is essential even in the earliest stages of learning to decode words with simple consonant-vowel-consonant words (*l-o-t*; *m-a-n*). It is also important much later when dealing with multi-syllabic words (*re-mem-ber*; *cal-cu-la-tor*).

> *Segmentation*

This means analysing sentences into words, words into syllables, and syllables into separate sounds. It is useful to stretch words out as we say them slowly, so that the separate sound units can be heard. The earliest segmentation involves separating the beginning sound (onset) from the vowel and consonants unit that follows (rime) in a single-syllable word. For example: *p – ost, tr – uck, b – ench, sl – eep*. Rime units are the basis for many word families such as *lick, sick, kick, pick, wick, trick, stick*. Practice in onset and rime activities can help students grasp the value of processing groups of letters together, rather than sounding out each single letter. Tunmer et al. (2002, p. 18) have observed, 'To discover mappings between spelling patterns and sound patterns, children must be able to segment spoken words into subcomponents'.

> *Isolation*

This means identifying the initial, final and medial sounds in a target word.

Many commercially published phonological training programs are available – for example, Blachman et al. (2000) and Goldsworthy (2001).

Teaching phonics and decoding

Teaching phonics means teaching learners the precise relationships between letters and groups of letters and the sounds they represent, and how to use this knowledge to decode or spell unfamiliar words. Research evidence very strongly supports direct and systematic instruction in phonic knowledge to be provided soon after the child reaches the age of 5 (Ehri et al., 2001a;

National Reading Panel, 2000; Tunmer et al., 2002). This early start provides a firm foundation on which to build higher-order literacy skills.

Over the years, several different ways of teaching phonics have been developed (Ehri et al., 2001a). These include:

> Analytic phonics
Letter-to-sound relationships are taught by breaking down words already known by sight into their separate phonic components: e.g. *stop* = /st/ − /o/ − /p/.

> Synthetic phonics
Letter-to-sound correspondences are explicitly taught and practised first, and this knowledge is then used to sound-out and blend words in print (e.g. /t/ − /a/ − /p/ = *tap*. The process of blending a sequence of sounds successfully is the main focus in this method. The initial learning of basic letter–sound correspondences is facilitated if children are required to write the letter at the same time as they say the sound (Sumbler & Willows, 1996) and some programs teach letter formation (handwriting) in tandem with phonics.

> Embedded phonics
This means using a combined analytic and synthetic approach to learn phonic units by decoding unfamiliar words that are met within paragraphs of meaningful text. This is less systematic (and therefore potentially less effective) than either of the above approaches.

> Phonics through spelling
Children can learn a great deal about letter-to-sound correspondences as they attempt to spell the words they need as they write. 'I want to write *stop*. How does it begin? /S/... /S-t/ ... /o/ ... /p/. *Stop*. OK. That looks good'. Again, the efficacy of this method is much less certain than the explicit teaching involved in synthetic and analytic phonics.

Currently, synthetic phonics has most support from research and is recommended as the approach of choice for beginning reading (Coltheart & Prior, 2006; Ehri et al, 2001a; Johnston & Watson, 2005; Macmillan,

2003; Mesmer & Griffith 2006). It has been advocated as best practice in various key reports on the teaching of reading in Australia, the United Kingdom and the United States of America (e.g., DEST, 2005; National Reading Panel, 2000; Rose, 2006). It appears that the synthetic approach is equally effective regardless of whether it uses single-letter decoding or teaches students to recognise and blend larger units such as digraphs and other common letter groups (Aaron et al., 1999; Tan et al., 2007).

For most children, the order in which they learn letter-to-sound correspondences is not important. But when working with students who have difficulties mastering phonics it is often helpful to consider how the most basic 26 single letter-to-sound correspondences might best be organised into a logical teaching sequence (Heilman, 2006). One might begin, for example, by selecting highly contrastive sounds such as /m/, /k/, /v/ each with a quite different lip or tongue position, and avoiding confusable sounds such as /m/ and /n/, or /p/ and /b/. It is also help-ful to teach first the most consistent and common single letter–sound associations.

But single letter-to-sound correspondences are only the very first step in mastering phonics. In the English language we have 26 letters of the alphabet but there are approximately 44 speech sounds that need to be represented in print. It is therefore necessary to teach children the groups of letters used in combination (orthographic units) that are required to represent the other sounds. These combinations include *digraphs* which are two letters together that represent a single speech sound (e.g. *ch, th, sh, ph, wh, –ck, –gh*; *consonant blends* such as *tr–, bl, sw, cr*, etc., and larger units such as *prefixes, suffixes* and other units, for example, *pre–, un–, –tion, –est, –ing*. For the highest level of proficiency in recognising and spelling unfamiliar words, children need to be competent in working with longer and more complex letter-strings. In addition, there are numerous *vowel digraphs* and *diphthongs* that often give children problems when reading and spelling, these include *ai, ie, ar, oa, oi, oo, au, ea, ee, ou, ue, oy*. These units are best taught and practised in the context of word families, where words sharing the common feature are compared and contrasted.

Once children have acquired functional decoding skills, and once they have built an adequate sight vocabulary, becoming fluent at word identification involves storing in memory relevant connections between common *groups of letters* within words and their pronunciation (e.g. *−eed*, *−eat*, *−tch*, *−ing*, *dis−*, *pro−*) (de Jong & Share, 2007; Ehri, 1997). The guidelines of the National Accelerated Literacy Program operating in several parts of Australia state that:

> While students need to learn phonics, they also need to learn to look for the larger letter patterns in English that facilitate automatic decoding. They have to make the transition from 'sounding out' to fast automatic recognition of letter pattern chunks. (NALP, 2007, n.p.)

The evidence seems to be that, with frequent practice in reading, children making normal progress will begin to store these letter patterns that will help them identify and spell other words. An effective teaching program will provide all children with opportunities for 'word study', in which words are compared and contrasted, analysed and decomposed into their parts. Word study helps raise students' awareness of common orthographic units (Donnell, 2007; Williams & Phillips-Birdsong, 2006). In addition to reading practice and word study, giving due attention to accurate spelling when writing is known to aid the acquisition of orthographic knowledge (Castles & Nation, 2008; Shahar-Yames & Share, 2008).

There are many programs designed to teach phonic knowledge in a very systematic way. One of the most useful and manageable is *THRASS* (*Teaching Handwriting, Reading and Spelling Skills*: Davies & Ritchie, 2004). This program is designed to teach children how specific letters and letter groups represent the 44 phonemes in the English language. Approaches such as *THRASS* use direct teaching and are therefore highly appropriate for children with learning difficulties who otherwise remain confused about the fact that the same sound units in English can sometimes be represented by different letter groups (e.g. *− ight* and *−ite*) and how an identical letter combination can represent different sounds (e.g. /ow/ as in *flower* or /ow/ as in *snow*).

Another very successful program is *Jolly Phonics* (Lloyd & Wernham, 1995). *Jolly Phonics* uses the synthetic phonic method to teach basic sound-to-letter correspondences using, in the early stages, a multi-sensory approach.

As a guiding principle, phonic knowledge and decoding skills should not be taught and practised totally out of context. Phonic skills are only functional if they help with the reading and writing of meaningful text − which is why those who argue against a balanced approach to reading instruction seem to be missing the point. While students do need specific time devoted to mastering phonic units and working with word families, every effort must be made to ensure that this learning is also applied to authentic reading and writing. In addition to direct instruction in phonics, much phonic knowledge can be taught and reinforced from words children are reading in their books or are attempting to write.

Improving word recognition

For reading to become swift and automatic, students need to move beyond the level of phonic decoding to recognise most words instantly by sight (Prior, 1996). All 'irregular' words – that is, words that do not use logical letter-to-sound relationships and cannot be decoded by sounding the letters (for example, *said, any, the, are*) – must of course be mastered by sight. Many of the most frequently used words in print are in this category. Students who have problems committing words to long-term memory require a teaching program that provides much repetition and overlearning of text material. For students with severe reading difficulties, Neill (2005) suggests that progress can be made by using a multi-sensory approach to word learning involving kinaesthetic activities such as tracing, writing, typing and highlighting words with colour. Attention also needs to be focused on identifying syllables, writing a word from memory and studying word families.

The use of flashcards to practise the overlearning of key words through frequent exposure has been a long-established practice in early reading and in remedial programs (Nicholson, 1998) and can be particularly helpful for learning irregular words that cannot be decoded using phonics. Similarly, computer programs that present these words frequently on the screen and require the learner to type the word several times can also be helpful. However, Aaron et al. (1999) suggest that specific activities of this visual and visual-motor memorisation type may not be effective in the longer term unless the student can also recognise phonological cues within irregular words and can attend to word meanings.

Bruce and Robinson (2002) explored the feasibility of using a meta-cognitive approach to teaching word identification skills to upper primary low-progress readers. The students were taught to use three possible strategies:

▶ Consider the context in which the word appears (semantic and syntactic cues).
▶ Compare the word with other known words (phonemic and orthographic cues).
▶ 'Carve up' the word into chunks (morphological cues).

They also taught the students to be flexible in attacking words, to look for cues to meaning and pronunciation, and to ask themselves if the word makes sense in this context? The most effective strategies were found to be 'carve up the word' and 'compare with a known word'.

Similarly, Lovett et al. (2000) also recognised the potential value of teaching readers to become more independent in their ability to identify unfamiliar words. Their program called *WIST (Word Identification Strategy Training)* adopts a metacognitive 'self-talk' approach and teaches students to check whether they can identify a word by:

▶ analogy with known words
▶ identification of part of the word
▶ trying different pronunciations of the word
▶ peeling off prefixes and suffixes.

Interestingly, Lovett et al. (2000) also discovered that students in the study made maximum progress when a *PHAB/DI (Phonological Analysis and Blending: Direct Instruction)* program was used together with the *WIST* strategy-training program.

Metacognitive self-regulatory approaches of the type described above may be feasible with students in upper primary and secondary schools, but younger children may not have developed sufficient metacognitive awareness. However, encouraging all beginning readers to think carefully about any word they can't immediately recognise, and to try various ways to work it out, will help raise their skills above a 'look and guess' level.

Word recognition as the prerequisite for comprehension

Identifying words in print is thus the most basic but indispensable first step toward reading connected text with understanding. Meaning can only be derived from text if the words can be swiftly and easily recognised. Fluent word recognition releases the reader's cognitive abilities to concentrate fully on the meaning of the material being read and his or her response to it.

The skills described in this chapter provide the essential starting point for effective instruction for all beginning readers. They also represent the top priority areas for attention in most remedial or intervention programs for struggling readers in the primary school years. The next chapter explores the comprehension difficulties encountered by some students. Many of these students have developed adequate word recognition skills, but still have problems.

LINKS TO MORE ON SIMPLE VIEW OF READING

▶ Wren (2003) provides a very clear description of the simple view of reading and its potential value online at: http://www.balancedreading. com/simple.html
▶ Catts et al. (2003) online at: http://www2.ku.edu/~splh/Catts/poster7. pdf

LINKS TO MORE ON DEVELOPING WORD RECOGNITION ABILITY

▶ Word recognition strategies are discussed at: http://www.eduplace.com/ rdg/res/teach/rec.html
▶ Additional information on the teaching of word recognition skills is available at: http://literacy.kent.edu/nto/manual02/Section4_BasicSkills. pdf
▶ The Blumberg Centre at the Indiana State University provides much useful advice on teaching word recognition, phonemic awareness and phonics. http://www.indstate.edu/soe/blumberg/reading/rd-word.html

LINKS TO MORE ON SYNTHETIC PHONICS

▶ An overview of phonics instruction is provided at: http://www.ltscotland.org.uk/5to14/specialfocus/earlyintervention/issues/phonics.asp

▶ Research evidence of the effectiveness of synthetic phonics is summarised at: http://www.jollylearning.co.uk/research2.htm

▶ The Communication, Language and Literacy Development section of the UK Standards website provides valuable guidance on phonics instruction, including the early phonics program *Letters and Sounds* (2008). Available online at: http://www.standards.dfes.gov.uk/local/clld/las.html

▶ The OFSTED report (June 2008) *Teacher trainees and phonics: An evaluation of the response of providers of initial teacher training to the recommendations of the Rose Review* is available online at: http://www.ofsted.gov.uk/assets/Internet_Content/Shared_Content/IIFD/Files/Initial%20teacher%20education%20and%20phonics.doc

Reading difficulties at text level

KEY ISSUES

▶ **Comprehension:** Reading a text with full understanding draws on the reader's background experience, general knowledge, vocabulary, syntactical awareness and word identification skills.

▶ **Comprehension difficulties:** Some difficulties are related directly to poor word recognition skills; but other factors can also create problems.

▶ **Online reading comprehension:** Online texts offer readers a new set of challenges – and a new set of opportunities.

▶ **Fluency and comprehension:** A reciprocal relationship exists between these two components of reading ability.

Referring again to the simple view of reading, the second essential component is comprehension. It is obviously not sufficient that a reader can recognise words on a page – the words, taken together, must make sense and must convey information. Explicit instruction in word recognition and decoding, as described in the previous chapter, must be accompanied from the start by the explicit teaching of comprehension skills and strategies (Ehri et al., 2007; Rapp et al., 2007).

In order to understand text, a reader must be able to identify words rapidly, know the meaning of almost all of the words, and be able to combine sequential units of meaning into a coherent message. Naturally, the majority of students who are very weak at word recognition will have serious difficulties with comprehension. But, it is recognised now that some students who develop adequate word-reading ability and fluency still have difficulty understanding what they are reading, particularly when faced with the expository style of writing used within many school textbooks (Cain & Oakhill, 2006). Some 10 per cent to 15 per cent of students are reported to exhibit this problem (Walczyk & Griffith-Ross, 2007); and Woolley (2007) suggests that many are not detected until they are in upper primary school. Providing intervention so late is usually not very effective because by then secondary reactions to failure have set in to undermine students' confidence and motivation (Ziolkowska, 2007). Students who don't understand much of what they read are likely to turn away from books (Gersten et al., 2001).

This chapter explores the nature of reading comprehension and addresses some of the factors associated with students' problems in understanding text. Chapter 4 describes some of the instructional practices that can be used to improve comprehension.

Defining and describing reading comprehension

Reading comprehension can be defined as an active thinking process through which a reader intentionally constructs meaning to form a deeper understanding of concepts and information presented in a text (Blanton et al., 2007; Neufeld 2006; Rapp et al., 2007). To comprehend, readers must use information they already possess to filter, interpret, organise and reflect upon the incoming information from the page. Efficient interpretation of text involves a combination of word recognition skills, linking of new information to prior knowledge, and application of appropriate strategies such as locating the main idea, making connections, questioning, inferring and predicting. McCardle et al. (2002) suggest that comprehension pro-cesses draw on many cognitive and linguistic abilities – most notably, vocabulary, recalling background knowledge, sentence processing, verbal reasoning, knowledge of print conventions and working memory. Weak-ness in any of these abilities can impair reading comprehension and can cause a student to disengage from the task of interpreting text.

Reading comprehension is often conceptualised as functioning at different levels of sophistication and referred to, for example, as *literal, inferential* and *critical*. The most basic level (literal) is where the reader is able to understand the factual information presented in a passage of text – for example, he or she can tell you the name of the main character and what he does for a living, because that information is stated explicitly in the text. The next level is referred to as the inferential level. At this level the reader is able to go beyond the words on the page and infer other details – for example, to realise that the main character is angry from what he says and what he does. Being able to operate at the inferential level means that the reader is using information effectively to deduce cause and effect, and to anticipate what may come next. At a more demanding level (critical reading), the reader is able to appraise what he or she is reading – for example, detecting good writing style from the author, recognising when some statements in the text are biased or incorrect, appreciating the writer's viewpoint, comparing and contrasting information with other facts they have read elsewhere, and reflecting upon the importance or otherwise of the opinions presented. Weak readers who are still struggling with word recognition have enormous difficulty progressing beyond a literal level of comprehension because most of their cognitive effort is taken up in unlocking the print.

Good and poor comprehenders

Readers who are good comprehenders use a variety of cognitive skills as they read. For example, as they process narrative material they may create mental pictures (visualise scenes, actions and characters); they may reflect critically upon the relevance of what they are reading; they may seek answers to questions; they may challenge the accuracy of stated facts; and they monitor their own level of understanding. They are also able to summarise the main points in what they have read. In other words, effective readers are able to put information together, make connections, remember and retell facts, evaluate what they read, and substantiate their opinions, conclusions and predictions (Thomas et al., 2008). They use metacognition to monitor their own level of understanding as they read, and often they will modify their approach by, for example, pausing to go back and read again a particular sentence or paragraph, or checking the meaning of a word in the glossary or online dictionary. Proficient readers are flexible in that they adjust their reading strategies as a function of the difficulty of the text, their familiarity with the topic, the structure (cohesion) of the material, and their goals in reading it.

According to Torgesen (2000), reading comprehension is both a cognitive and an affective activity. Good readers are 'active' in the sense of becoming involved cognitively and emotionally in what they are reading. They are often keen to use text as a way of obtaining new information, acquiring new ideas, solving problems, and as a source of enjoyment.

Weak comprehenders, on the other hand, display few of the positive attributes typical of good readers. Their laborious and slow identification of words on the page makes comprehension very difficult and causes the experience of reading to be tedious and frustrating. They seem unable to connect ideas together as they read, and they remember very little of the details after they have read a passage (Ricketts et al., 2008; Weekes et al., 2008). Weak readers do not think deeply about what they are reading, do not interact cognitively with the information, and do not monitor their own level of understanding. Often, they do not check back or re-read the material when meaning is lost (Sencibaugh, 2007), and they are poor at inferring meaning beyond the words given on the page. Weak readers tend not to read critically or attend sufficiently to details (Cragg & Nation, 2006). Some readers seem to lose sight of the fact that what they are reading is supposed to make sense; so when it doesn't make sense they make no attempt to re-read or self-correct. The difficulties for most poor readers are compounded by the fact that they do not possess effective strategies to help them interpret and interact with text.

Causes of poor comprehension

Comprehension problems can be caused by a variety of different factors, including those intrinsic to the individual and others related to insufficient instruction or to inappropriate materials. The eight most frequently mentioned causal factors are summarised below, together with brief implications for instruction.

> Limited vocabulary knowledge

Studies have confirmed that reading comprehension is closely related to a student's level of spoken language competence (Hummel, 2000; Kemple et al., 2008). For example, Myers and Botting (2008) studied the language and literacy skills of 11-year-old students in an inner-city disadvantaged school in the United Kingdom. They found that 58 per cent of these students had comprehension problems closely related to poor oral language skills.

If a student has difficulty understanding what he or she is reading, it is worth considering whether there is a serious mismatch between the student's own knowledge of word meanings (expressive and listening vocabulary) and the words used in the text. The student may be able to read a word correctly on the page but not know its meaning – for example, in the sentence 'The farmer inspected his crops growing in the next field', the child who has never encountered the word 'crop' before may think it is a particular type of vegetable or fruit. There is obviously a need sometimes to pre-teach new vocabulary before a text is read in order to enhance comprehension. There is also a need to devote more time to vocabulary development as an integral part of the classroom literacy program.

> Lack of fluency

There are high correlations between oral reading fluency and comprehension (Carver, 2000; Klinger et al., 2007). There appears to be an optimum rate of fluency in reading that allows for accurate processing of information. Automaticity in reading, based mainly on smooth and effortless word identification and contextual cueing, allows the reader to use all available cognitive capacity to focus on meaning. Students who read very slowly – or much too fast – often comprehend poorly. Slow reading tends to restrict cognitive capacity to the low-level processing of letters and words rather than allowing full attention to be devoted to higher-order ideas and concepts within the text. But very fast reading may result in inaccurate word recognition, and important details being overlooked. Sometimes, attention to rate of reading needs to be a specific focus in students' literacy programs, particularly in terms of increasing fluency and expression of those who read much too slowly (Allington, 2001).

> *Lack of familiarity with the subject matter*

It is much easier to read with understanding if the reader already possesses some prior knowledge of the topic (Gersten et al., 2001; Kemple et al., 2008). Using the school textbook as the medium for first introducing new information to students is not usually the most effective method of delivery. It is better to provide information first by other means (e.g. video, posters, mini-lecture, discussion) to build firm background knowledge before students are expected to read about that theme in printed texts. This is particularly important for weaker readers.

> *Difficulty level of the text (readability)*

The difficulty level of text is a major factor influencing whether or not material can be read with understanding (Fountas & Pinnell, 2006). Text that is complex in terms of concepts, vocabulary, sentence length and structure is difficult for readers to process. For this reason, expository text – with its facts, detailed descriptions, explanations, definitions, sequences, cause and effect relationships, and comparisons – is much more difficult to process than narrative text (Gersten et al., 2001; Thomas et al., 2008).

Conventional wisdom suggests that one way to assist struggling readers is to ensure that the difficulty level of the texts they are required to read is compatible with their current reading ability. In other words, it has always been accepted that the weaker the reader, the easier the book needs to be to ensure success. Books that are too difficult (at 'frustration level') will cause a reader to make too many errors. Books that are suitable for a student to read independently should have an error rate of less than 5 per cent. If a student is reading with a partner or being directly tutored by an adult, the potential error rate can be slightly higher because immediate correction is available ('instructional level'). Intervention programs such as *Reading Recovery* (Clay, 1993) and *Multilit* (Pearce et al., 2006; Wheldall & Beaman, 2007) rely on the careful matching of texts to students' existing skills. However, a few recent research studies have yielded information suggesting that using books a little above the reader's present reading level can be useful for advancing reading skills if the student's attempts are *effectively supported* and if they are given help with interpretation (Cramer & Rosenfeld, 2008; Ehri, et al., 2007; Gray & Cowey, 2005; Thomas et al., 2008).

> Inadequate use of effective reading strategies

Unlike skilled readers, weaker readers do not approach the interpretation of text strategically. They tend not to know of, or use, strategies that would help them visualise, make connections, reflect, infer, predict, question and summarise (Kemple et al., 2008; McKown & Barnett, 2007; Sencibaugh, 2007). Nor do they self-monitor and self-correct. There is an urgent need to teach these students how to approach text systematically and critically. Pressley (2006) argues that the goal of literacy teaching should be to develop fully self-regulated readers who are skilled and strategic in reading for meaning. He challenges the belief held by many teachers that students improve in comprehension ability if they simply do massive amounts of reading and answer comprehension tests. Pressley suggests that strategy training to enhance comprehension and study skills should be an essential part of any balanced approach to literacy teaching. There is much evidence to support such a view (e.g., Berninger et al., 2003; De Lemos, 2005; Magliano et al., 1999; Woolley, 2007). Unfortunately, there is evidence that reading is not being taught as a thinking activity and many teachers do not spend much time (sometimes *no time*) instructing students in the use of comprehension strategies (Blanton et al., 2007; McKown & Barnett, 2007).

> Weak verbal reasoning

The ability to understand text, and particularly to go beyond the words on the page in order to make relevant connections among facts and to critique the ideas, reflects the operation of verbal reasoning (Cain & Oakhill, 2006; Hummel, 2000). To some extent, the ability to reason is determined by an individual's level of intelligence; but guided reading activities in which a teacher uses effective questioning to challenge students to think more deeply about the text they are reading are helpful in developing their ability to reason from the information given. Deliberately guiding students to make connections between new information in text and their existing bank of knowledge is beneficial.

> Problems with processing information

In order to maintain the meaning of text as the sentences and paragraphs accumulate, a reader has to be able to keep relevant information within working memory and make necessary connections between ideas (Cohen-Mimran & Sapir, 2007; Savage et al., 2007; Swanson & Jerman, 2007). Limited working memory is sometimes suggested as a causal factor in poor comprehension. It is known that individuals differ in their working-memory capacity, with some able to process and accommodate much more information than others. Working-memory capacity is significantly reduced if an individual is stressed or anxious, or is preoccupied and distracted by other issues. But it is also clear that slow word-by-word reading places unreasonable demands on working-memory span and makes it almost impossible to store information long enough for meaning to be maintained.

The implications for teaching are that slow readers should be encouraged to re-read material, several times if necessary, in order to process the information successfully. It is also necessary to reduce factors that may be causing a reader to be anxious or distracted and to ensure that the student is giving due attention to the task. Hall and Harding (2003) have identified attention (active engagement) and self-regulation as important influences on reading with understanding.

> Problems in recalling information after reading

Recall is dependent partly upon factors such as vividness and relevance of the information in the text; but it is also dependent upon a student giving adequate attention to the reading task and knowing that it is important to remember details. Recall is strongest when readers connect new information in the text to their previous knowledge and experience, and when they rehearse key points from the text (Chan & Dally, 2002; Myers & Botting, 2008; Sencibaugh, 2007). The use of graphic organisers to summarise and consolidate key points before, during and after reading can also help to strengthen recall of information (Sabbatino, 2004). Effective intervention for comprehension usually involves activities that help students allocate attention selectively to relevant aspects of the text so that it is easier to remember key information (Fuchs et al., 1997). It can also be noted in passing that there is some evidence to suggest that certain students with a learning disability have an abnormally slow rate of processing and retrieving information from long-term memory (Heath et al., 2006). In such cases, teachers need to give adequate time for the student to respond before assuming lack of knowledge.

Comprehending online material

The online document *Standards for teachers of English language and literacy in Australia (STELLA)* (AATE/ALEA, 2001) states that: 'Literacy is the flexible and sustainable mastery of a repertoire of practices with the texts of traditional and new communications technology via spoken language, print and multimedia'. This definition reminds us that literacy skills are increasingly brought into play in contexts other than books and print. Issues related to comprehending verbal and graphic material presented in other media need to be considered.

We have reached the stage in this age of information technology where many students spend more time engaging with text on a computer screen than they do engaging with books and print. Onscreen text presents its own challenges and opportunities for increasing comprehension skills. O'Brien et al. (2007) suggest that computers and online information provide an opportunity to teach literacy skills in an age-appropriate and mature manner, without the need for a formal drill-and-practice remedial approach. This makes computer-mode presentations particularly appropriate when working with disenchanted secondary school students with reading difficulties, and with adults. Online resources such as websites, Wikipedia, email and computer games can all provide meaningful reading activities that are motivating and relevant. Applying comprehension strategies to text via such media can be motivating and can build a feeling of competence in the learner.

For students to read and comprehend online material effectively, and to search for and locate information, they require certain specific entry knowledge and skills (Coiro & Dobler, 2007; Le Bigot & Rouet, 2007). In particular they need:

- adequate keyboard skills and other basic computer competencies
- knowledge of typical website structures
- knowledge of search-engine functions
- inferential reasoning strategies
- note-taking skills
- ability to detect bias, and to judge the trustworthiness of stated information (is it fact or opinion?)
- self-regulation.

Material already exists to help students apply their knowledge and skills to computer technology to obtain and use information. For example, *WebQuest* is an inquiry-based activity that requires learners to interact with resources on the Internet to collect and collate data (Dodge, 1995; Skylar et al., 2007). It requires basic computer skills, and when used with weaker readers, the activity needs to be carefully structured so that learners do not become frustrated by failure to locate information or to be overloaded by what they do find. Teachers can adapt *WebQuest* by providing students with step-by-step procedures, prepared response sheets and graphic organisers to which students can add information as they locate and summarise it.

Of course, a computer mode of presentation can also enhance other aspects of reading. For example, 'talking books' have become popular for presenting stories and other literary forms to readers. According to Oakley (2002, p. 20):

> Electronic talking books, also known as 'electronic storybooks', are usually stories that are augmented by a sound track, graphics and often animation. Readers can opt to have texts read aloud to them electronically by fluent, expressive readers. Words, phrases or sentences may be highlighted as they are narrated by the computer, allowing readers to track the text with their eyes. By clicking on particular words, readers can often access pronunciations, pictorial representations of words, or definitions.

As an example, Oakley (2002) found that boys in Year 4 benefited in terms of fluency and expression from practising repeated readings along with the talking book. However, she did identify some constraints in such a medium, including difficulty in locating e-texts at an appropriate reading level and of a suitable length. It was also found that highlighting text as it is read on the screen can inhibit normal eye movements while reading. In some cases, animations inserted in the e-book interrupt the flow of the story. Even given these potential constraints, talking books are assuming an important place within comprehensive language and literacy programs (Benke, 2000; Kennedy, 2000).

Reciprocal relationship between fluency and comprehension

Fluency is actually a reflection of a reader's competence in rapid word recognition, supported by a good understanding of what is being read. Poor word recognition skills lead to dysfluent reading performance and loss of meaning. We cannot read fluently any text that we do not understand; but we can read text much more fluently when we do understand it. Dysfluent reading may therefore signal to the teacher that the text a student is using contains vocabulary and concepts that are beyond the reader's current capabilities.

Very occasionally, a student's lack of fluency may be due to an underlying weakness in retrieving known words from memory (dysnomia – the 'word-finding difficulty' referred to earlier); but this is usually only a factor in students with a specific learning disability (Schilling et al., 2007). Most dysfluency is caused by lack of reading practice, inefficient word recognition skills, and trying to read books that are too difficult.

Fluency develops as a direct result of a reader establishing a fully functional sight vocabulary, good decoding skills and effective use of context. Fluency only develops with abundant practice in reading, both silently and aloud. One of the most important aims in literacy programs, mainstream and remedial, is to help students achieve greater fluency in their reading (Kairaluoma et al., 2007; Le Vasseu et al., 2008). Oral reading fluency (ORF) can be measured reasonably accurately to provide some evidence of improvement over time (Hasbrouck & Tindal, 2006).

Repeated Reading is one teaching procedure used to increase fluency, accuracy, expression and confidence (Mandlebaum et al., 2007). It simply requires readers to practise reading a short passage aloud until success rate is above 95 per cent and the material can be read aloud fluently. Repeated Reading, if coupled with questioning and discussion after reading, can improve comprehension (Therrien et al., 2006). Allington (2001) reviewed a number of studies evaluating the effectiveness of repeated reading and concludes that repeated readings of a text are particularly effective in fostering greater confidence and more fluent reading in students with reading difficulties.

In a remedial reading situation, Repeated Reading practice usually follows these steps:

▶ teacher first models the reading while the student follows in the text

▶ teacher spends a few minutes making sure that the student fully understands the material

▶ student then practises reading the material aloud several times with corrective feedback from the teacher

▶ student continues to practise until nearly perfect

▶ student finally records the reading on tape and then listens to his or her own fluent performance.

In summary, reading comprehension problems can be minimised by providing students with texts at an appropriate level of difficulty (or if a more difficult text must be used, by providing all necessary support), pre-teaching any difficult vocabulary, ensuring that word recognition and decoding skills are mastered, devoting sufficient time to reading practice, and teaching effective comprehension strategies. Some examples of such strategies are presented in the following chapter.

LINKS TO MORE ON READING COMPREHENSION

▶ Resources and ideas for improving reading comprehension available online at: http://www.readingcomprehensionconnection.com/lesson.php

▶ An excellent article on comprehension by Michael Pressley (2000) available online at: http://www.readingonline.org/articles/handbook/pressley/index.html

▶ A document by Jan Baumel (2008) pulls together decoding, vocabulary building and reading comprehension strategies. Available online at: http://www.schwablearning.org/articles.aspx?r=499

▶ *Improving fluency in young readers.* A concise and readable summary of key points. Available online at: http://www.busyteachercafe.com/units/fluency.htm

▶ *Developing reading fluency.* Some relevant background information and practical suggestions. Available online at: http://www.auburn.edu/~murraba/fluency.html

four

Interventions for reading

▶ **Improving comprehension:** Explicit instruction in comprehension strategies can greatly increase students' ability to understand both narrative and expository texts.

▶ **Classroom organisation:** Peer tutoring has proved to be very effective for increasing literacy achievement.

▶ **Large-scale literacy interventions:** This chapter summarises several interventions operating at system level in Australia and the United States of America.

Teachers' ingenuity, together with evidence from classroom research, has contributed to the wide range of available methods and activities that can foster reading and writing skills and can boost the attainment of weaker readers. This chapter provides an overview of a few approaches, ranging from those that can be implemented with individuals or with small groups of students, through to a brief summary of those that are operating on a much larger scale across schools. The Links box contains information on sources for other ideas and models.

Teaching comprehension skills and strategies

Research in the past two decades has focused attention on intervention methods for enhancing students' comprehension. Results indicate that it is certainly possible to teach students more effective ways of increasing their understanding of text (e.g., Ellis, 2005; Neufeld, 2006; Pressley & Hilden, 2006; Swanson, 2000). Strategies such as previewing text before reading, self-questioning, self-monitoring, rehearsing information, constructing graphic organisers to connect ideas and overtly summarising key points, have all proved valuable. Rapp et al. (2007, p. 307) state: 'Comprehension instruction is an attempt to teach students how to think while they read.'

But, teaching reading comprehension strategies is not particularly easy. Williams (2005, p. 6) correctly informs us that, 'Strategies are notoriously difficult to teach in a way that will ensure their effective use in authentic reading situations, and in addition, teaching teachers how to implement strategy instruction is often challenging'. Hay et al. (2005) report that students with learning difficulties stand to benefit most from strategy instruction, but they take even longer than other students to master the steps and to use them independently. For this reason, the training in strategy use should not be abandoned too quickly. Weaker readers need much practice to reach a stage where they can become independent and self-regulating (Horner & O'Connor, 2007). It is also necessary to devise strategies that are not too complex. The more steps involved in a strategy, the less likely it is that weaker readers will remember to use them.

The effective teaching of a strategic approach to comprehension requires firstly direct explanation and clear demonstration by the teacher. The teacher uses the techniques of 'thinking aloud' and 'self-questioning' while processing a typical passage of text and reflecting upon its meaning. This will need to be done several times, working with different texts. The value of using the strategy should be discussed with the class, and students must be given abundant time for guided practice in applying the same strategy and using the same self-talk with feedback from the teacher.

In addition to teacher-directed instruction, an effective program for enhancing comprehension skills should include large amounts of time devoted to reading for information, together with frequent occasions when students can talk with their teacher and with one another about their response to a particular text (Thomas et al., 2008). Making meaning is a process that can be facilitated greatly by social interaction and discussion with teacher and in groups. This is sometimes referred to as 'text-based collaborative learning' (Biancrosa & Snow, 2006). Such activities should involve the use of a diversity of text types to increase readers' repertoire of analytical skills.

Sencibaugh's (2007) meta-analysis of reading intervention approaches shows that comprehension can indeed be improved when students are taught specifically to:

- self-monitor for understanding
- find the main idea in a paragraph
- self-question as they read
- make inferences and connections
- retell key information (e.g. restate the gist of a paragraph)
- summarise key points.

Other researchers have confirmed the value of focusing on these particular abilities (e.g., Boulware-Gooden et al., 2007; Hummel, 2000; Kemple et al., 2008; McKown & Barnett, 2007). Together they comprise a viable set of competencies to master.

In addition to the items above, Graham and Bellert (2005) include an emphasis on deeper analyses of text by looking for links or inconsistencies among the pieces of information, clarifying meanings, detecting the direction an argument may be taking, reading between the lines, recognising cause and effect relationships, and making predictions; all of these assist in the processes of making meaning. They also recommend encouraging students to visualise (create a mental picture) as they read narrative material, and to use graphic organisers for both narrative and expository texts to help map the main ideas, highlight key terms, make connections and summarise issues.

Examples of comprehension strategies

It can be seen from the examples below that most strategies tend to focus on activating prior knowledge, raising questions, making inferences or predictions, reading carefully to seek evidence to support or refute these predictions, and summarising or paraphrasing. Some strategies are based only on the text, while others also involve structured response sheets and may require students to write or to construct graphics such as story maps or tables. In teaching these reading strategies the teacher always plays a very active role and guides students in the desired direction by focused questioning that challenges their thinking.

> POSSE

This strategy was used successfully with grade 4, 5 and 6 students and deals with processing expository text. It is designed to activate students' prior knowledge about a topic and to link it with new information contained in the text (Englert & Mariage, 1991). A 'strategy sheet' is used to cover the five aspects listed below, and students add information to it in the form of a semantic map before, during and after the reading. The sheet provides a visual guide that provides direction and structure, linking what students already know with new information that is acquired while reading.

The five letters in the acronym POSSE stand for:

- **P**redict what issues will be covered in the text (based on your existing knowledge of the subject) and raise a question you want to answer
- **O**rganise your predicted points and question and link them into a semantic map
- **S**earch the text (read carefully to confirm or discredit your predictions)
- **S**ummarise the points gleaned from the reading
- **E**valuate your understanding of the text and what you have learned from it.

POSSE relies heavily on teacher modelling and thinking aloud, and even more on instructional dialogue between teacher and students and within the group of students.

> Directed Reading–Thinking Activity (DRTA)

DRTA has some features in common with POSSE. It is a whole-class instructional strategy designed to give students experience in previewing text before reading, predicting what an author may say, reading the narrative text to confirm or revise the predictions and elaborating upon responses (Snowball, 2005). Questioning by the teacher encourages the students to think analytically and critically about the subject matter they are reading. In order for some students with reading difficulties to get the most benefit from DRTA, it is usually necessary to have them re-read the passage, aiming for improved fluency so that cognitive effort can be redirected towards the meaning of the paragraphs.

The DRTA process involves three basic steps:

▶ predicting some of the information you may find, or raising some questions you hope to have answered in the text
▶ reading the text carefully, with your predictions and questions in mind
▶ being able to prove, with evidence from the text, any conclusions you make from your reading.

The teacher's involvement is mainly to ask focusing questions to activate students' prior knowledge and to stimulate thinking. For example: 'What do you think will happen? What is this likely to be about? How would she be feeling? Why do you think that? Can you prove what you say from something in the book?'

> The 3H strategy (Here – Hidden – or in my Head)

The purpose of this strategy for upper primary grades is to teach students where answers to specific questions may be found (Graham & Wong, 1993). The answer is either explicitly stated in the text (*here*), or is implied in the text and can be inferred if the reader thinks carefully about some information on the page (*hidden*), or the information is not on the page but is already in the student's prior knowledge (in the *head*) and needs to be recalled. In teaching the 3H strategy, students are cued to use appropriate text-based or knowledge-based information to answer questions. They are also taught to use self-questioning to help focus their own attention on selecting appropriate information and to monitor their own understanding. The teacher provides necessary prompting (e.g. the use of cue cards) in the beginning, but this support is faded out as students gain confidence and control of the strategy. The 3H strategy helps students appreciate that answers to questions are not necessarily stated explicitly within a text, and that often one must think carefully and go beyond the words.

The teaching sequence of the 3H strategy is as follows:

- Teacher poses a question related to the text.
- Teacher demonstrates (by 'thinking aloud') how to locate relevant information on the page (*here*).
- Students practise this step to find answers to additional questions, with feedback from the teacher.
- Teacher demonstrates the second possibility, using information on the page to infer or predict a possible answer (*hidden*).
- Students practise step 1 and step 2 together with guidance and feedback.
- Teacher demonstrates the third possibility, namely that the answer is not *here* or *hidden* but must be located from sources outside the text, for example from what a student already knows.
- Students practise step 1, step 2 and step 3 with guidance and feedback.
- Over the following lessons the strategy is reviewed and used again on a variety of text types.

> K-W-L strategy (Know – Want to know – Learned)

This strategy activates students' prior knowledge on a given topic, then invites them to generate some questions they hope the text may answer, and finally they must summarise any new information they have learned from the reading (Ogle, 1986). To facilitate this process, a 'KWL Chart' is provide for each student. The chart is ruled up with three columns, headed respectively 'what we *know*', 'what we *want to know*', and 'what we *learned*'. A fourth column might be added to the chart in which students can record their response to the material in the text; or they might write down suggestions for what they will do to make use of the information they have learned to extend their study of the same topic.

The KWL strategy is intended for use with expository texts, and the teacher needs to select material that lends itself well to this type of analysis. Expository text is more difficult than narrative text for students to understand, so the subject textbooks used in upper primary and secondary schools often cause problems. So too does the concise informative data presented online when students are conducting computer searches for their projects and assignments. Teachers and tutors need to appreciate the difficulties students experience with expository text. Most weaker readers need guidance to become more aware of the typical structure, style and sequence used within this type of text (Gersten et al., 2001; Williams, 2005).

The teaching sequence of the KWL strategy is as follows:

▶ Immediately before a non-fiction text is to be read, the students and teacher brainstorm and list all they know about the topic under the first column.

▶ Under the second column they generate some questions or issues that may be answered in the text.

▶ After reading the text, either silently or as a shared activity, the students write a dot-point summary in the third column listing the main things they have learned from the text.

General interventions

> *Narrative intervention*

For most readers, narrative text, with its settings, characters, actions, outcomes, and a conclusion is easier to read with understanding than expository text (Westerveld & Gillon, 2008). Most young children are familiar with narrative structure from having listened to stories read to them. However, researchers have discovered that some students with reading comprehension difficulties seem to have a poor grasp of typical story structure and can't use it to help them process, understand and remember information (Graham & Bellert, 2005). Narrative intervention teaches them explicitly about basic story elements such as:

▶ setting
▶ characters
▶ theme
▶ action
▶ resolution
▶ conclusion.

The teaching sequence for narrative intervention is as follows. Before starting a narrative reading the teacher can introduce (and record on the whiteboard) the characters and the setting, and can give some indication of the theme of the upcoming story. After the reading, students can retell the action, describe how the characters resolved any issues and state how the story ended. The teacher summarises his information on the board under the categories suggested above. The group then recaps on the story elements and uses the same framework to identify key aspects in other stories that are familiar to them. The framework can also be useful for helping students write narrative material (see Chapter 6).

> *Guided reading*

This important whole-class approach helps students become better comprehenders of different genres of text and better at processing and recalling important information. Guided reading can also foster students' vocabulary development. The approach can be introduced in simple ways in the junior primary years, and extended to more difficult texts throughout primary and secondary years (Fountas & Pinnell, 1996). Indeed, guided reading can help weaker readers cope much more successfully with textbooks in the secondary school.

Guided reading sessions place great importance on students' active participation and contribution in discussions, co-operative learning, and sharing of ideas and opinions. Guidance from the teacher is provided at three stages – before, during and after reading the text.

The teaching sequence for guided reading is as follows:

- **Before reading:** Guidance before reading prepares the reader to enter the text with some clear purpose and a plan of action in mind. At this stage the teacher may, for example, activate students' prior knowledge related to the topic, pre-teach some difficult vocabulary to be encountered in the text, encourage students to make predictions about information that may be presented, remind students of effective ways of processing and remembering information, and alert them to look out for certain points.
- **During reading:** Guidance during reading may encourage the student to look for cause and effect relationships, compare and contrast information, respond critically to information given, check for understanding, and highlight main ideas.
- **After reading the text:** The teacher may help students review information, summarise and retell, check for understanding, and encourage critical reflection and evaluation.

Partner reading and peer tutoring to enhance reading

Various models that involve students working together for purposes of reading skill development have been designed and evaluated. Evaluation of these models across a wide age range has produced positive results, showing that they can be very effective for increasing literacy skills (Fuchs et al., 1997; Kourea et al., 2007; McMaster et al., 2006). The options range from simply pairing students of the same reading ability together to engage in the reading of a specific text for practice purposes (partner reading), through to situations where one student teaches and provides corrective feedback to another (peer tutoring), and to more extensive use of students working together in class-wide peer tutoring (CWPT). In home tutoring situations a parent may take the role of partner.

Fuchs et al. (1997) developed a peer-assisted learning strategy (PALS) in which a higher-achieving student is paired with a lower-achieving student to complete various structured reading activities that help focus attention selectively on relevant aspects of text. The activities typically involve reading and retelling, making inferences and summarising paragraphs. Similarly, the peer-tutoring strategy used by Kourea et al. (2007) to improve word recognition and fluency in primary school students yielded positive results. Its additional benefits for the weaker reader included immediate feedback and correction, increased engagement with text, and more effective practice. In a project by Burns (2006), the student who would act as tutor for a weaker reader was taught to use a 'pause, prompt, praise' strategy, which in other studies has proved effective in encouraging weaker readers to persist with a reading task and to become more independent in decoding difficult words. Burns points out that, to be effective, peer tutoring has to be closely monitored by the teacher.

Literacy interventions at systems level: Australia

In Australia, where funding was made available in recent years to support projects and new initiatives in early literacy intervention, programs operating at systems level have included:

> *Reading Recovery*
This early intervention program was developed in New Zealand (Clay, 1993) and is now used in many other parts of the world. Children identified

as having reading difficulties after one year in school are placed in the program to receive intensive individual tuition every day for 30 minutes over one school term. The texts selected are designed to give the student a high success rate. Teachers keep 'running records' of children's oral reading performance and use these to target accurately the knowledge or strategies a student still needs to learn.

> SWELL (School-wide early language and literacy)

SWELL covers children from kindergarten into the early primary years and is a code-oriented beginning reading program (Center et al., 1998; Smith, 2001). It is based upon principles from the American intervention program *Success for All* (see below) and is for use within a whole-class setting. *SWELL* aims to prevent early failure by direct teaching of essential skills. For more information, see the Links box at the end of the chapter.

> CLaSS (Children's Literacy Success Strategy)

CLaSS is a whole-school approach that aims to maximise the literacy skills of all children in school years Prep to Grade 2 inclusive (Department of Education, Employment and Training, Victoria, 2001). The main components were derived from the Early Literacy Research Project (ELRP) in Victoria, which in turn had drawn inspiration from *Success for All*. Evaluation data support the value of this program in reducing reading difficulties (Crevola & Hill, 2005). See the Links box at the end of the chapter.

> PASS (Program of Additional Structure and Support)

This program is for P–2 children in Tasmania. Designed to provide significant support for at-risk children from Prep Class to Year 2. It is now subsumed under the more comprehensive *Flying Start Program*. See the Links box for details.

> Early Years Literacy Program

This program has operated in both Victoria and South Australia. In both states the focus is on providing effective instruction for students at the beginning stages of learning to read, with an emphasis also on professional development for teachers. See the Links box for details.

> *Multilit (Making Up Lost Time in Literacy)*

This program for students with reading difficulties in Year 2 and above focuses on decoding, sight vocabulary and text reading (Wheldall & Beaman, 2007). Emphasis is placed on selecting books carefully so that they are at an appropriate instructional level for the students concerned (Pearce et al., 2006).

> *Quick-Smart*

This is a research-based reading intervention for middle school students with learning difficulties (Graham et al., 2007). It involves structured 30-minute sessions to be conducted three times a week by a teacher or aide.

> *National Accelerated Literacy Program (NALP)*

NALP (previously named 'Scaffolded Literacy') targets minority group students (including mainly Indigenous students) and was piloted between 1998 and 2003 in five states and the territories (Cowey, 2007; Gray & Cowey, 2005). In 2004, Charles Darwin University in the Northern Territory took over the further implementation and evaluation of NALP. The program requires teachers to adopt an alternative way of teaching literacy by making the learning environment highly structured and supportive, and by making the purpose of every literacy activity explicit. The whole language approach is not successful with this population of students who need a clearly defined purpose for engaging in literacy acts. They benefit most from intensive, systematic, skills-based instruction (Emmett, 2007; Storry, 2007). Texts are used that are above the students' current ability level, but a great deal of guidance, scaffolding and direct teaching is provided. The text is studied intensively for word-level skills and meaning-level understanding. A high success rate is maintained to build confidence and motivation. The methodology is explained fully at the website (see the Links box at the end of the chapter).

Literacy interventions at systems level: United States of America

Literacy intervention programs in America are almost too numerous to mention. A brief description will be provided for three of the most comprehensive.

> *Success for All*

This early intervention approach involves intensive one-to-one teaching, using teachers or paraprofessionals to help increase the literacy skills of at-risk and socially disadvantaged children (Slavin & Madden, 2001). Lessons operate daily for 20 minutes. Emphasis is placed on the reading of meaningful material from the start, but due attention is also given to instruction in phonics and to teaching effective strategies for monitoring comprehension. Teachers involved in *Success for All* also participate in the regular classroom program to ensure that the one-to-one tutoring is closely linked to the mainstream literacy curriculum.

> *Enhanced Reading Opportunities Study*

This program targets secondary school students who are performing between 2 to 5 years below standard in literacy (Kemple et al., 2008). The project involves some 2900 Grade 9 students from 34 high schools. Groups of about 15 students are established to form small 'learning communities', and instruction is provided for a minimum of 225 minutes per week (over and above the time students spend in mainstream English classes). The program lasts approximately 8 months. Direct instruction in reading strategies is combined with student-centred and self-directed learning activities. Skills covered in the program include vocabulary development, phonic decoding, comprehension, fluency and writing. The comprehension strategies taught and practised include self-questioning, visual imagery, paraphrasing and inferring. Appropriate amounts of time are spent in silent sustained reading, discussing text, reflecting on key ideas, thinking aloud and writing responses. Two published reading programs designed specifically for adolescents are used for much of the course – *Reading Apprenticeship Academic Literacy* and *Xtreme Reading*. The designers of the project state that: 'The overarching goals of both programs are to help ninth-grade students adopt the strategies and routines used by proficient readers, improve their comprehension skills, and be motivated to read more and to enjoy reading' (Kemple et al., 2008, p. xii).

> *Reading Rescue*

This program was developed by the University of Florida and the Literacy Trust. It targets at-risk students in Grade 1 (Ehri et al., 2007). Instruction by teachers or paraprofessionals includes one-to-one tutoring in phonological awareness, systematic phonics, vocabulary, fluency and comprehension. Children are taught decoding and sight word recognition. They apply these skills to the reading of books that contain some degree of vocabulary control and contain a high proportion of decodable words. Questioning and discussion are used to develop comprehension of what is read.

Features of effective intervention

Torgesen (2007) and Pikulski (1997) highlight the fact that for intervention to be effective the students with difficulties need to be identified early and given intensive additional instruction. The key features of this additional instruction include:

▶ Reading for meaning is given top priority, with fluency as a major aim.
▶ Intervention sessions are frequent and sufficiently long to make a real difference to students' rate of learning.
▶ Instruction tends to be most effective in small groups.
▶ Books are selected carefully for readability level to ensure a high success rate.
▶ Word-level decoding skills are explicitly taught, with emphasis on recognising and using orthographic units.
▶ Writing is incorporated in the reading program to reinforce phonics, word recognition and sentence patterns.
▶ The pace of instruction is brisk.
▶ Assessment of learning is ongoing, and the data collected from assessment guides teachers' decision making.
▶ A strong link is forged between home and school for continuity of program.

In the next chapter attention will be given to the other key element of literacy, namely the ability to write. Just as problems can arise with learning to read, so too difficulties can easily occur in acquiring functional writing skills.

LINKS TO MORE ON SPECIFIC INTERVENTIONS

▶ Many useful items on reading comprehension, vocabulary development, and strategy training are available online at: http://www.literacy.uconn.edu/compre.htm

▶ Information about the early intervention program SWELL can be located online at: http://www.mn.catholic.edu.au/index.cfm?menukey=80 and at http://mn.catholic.edu.au/projects/evaluation.pdf

▶ A full description of the National Accelerated Literacy program is presented in the following websites:
http://www.nalp.edu.au/documents/NALPpromobookletfinal_000.pdf
http://www.nalp.edu.au/whatisnalp.htm
http://www.nalp.edu.au/docs/Reflections_Amata_School.pdf

▶ Information on Children's Literacy Success Strategy (ClaSS) is available online at: http://web.cecv.vic.catholic.edu.au/publications/literacy/focus.pdf

▶ For information on PASS (*Program of Additional Structure and Support*) in Tasmania, see Overton, J. (2001). *Mapping literacy in Tasmania*. Online literature review available from: http://www.aare.edu.au/01pap/ove01171.htm

▶ Early Years Literacy Program. Information online at: http://www.earlyyearsliteracy.sa.edu.au/pages/cg0001086/19256/

▶ From the Commonwealth Government Department of Education, Science and Training, *MyRead: Strategies for teaching reading in middle years*. Available online at: http://www.myread.org/index.htm

Difficulties with writing and spelling

▶ **The process of writing:** Writing can be extremely demanding for students because it calls upon many experiential, cognitive, linguistic, affective and psycho-motor memories and abilities.

▶ **Simple view of writing:** Writing involves lower-order transcription skills and higher-order composing skills.

▶ **Affective reactions to writing difficulties:** The problems experienced by weaker writers are compounded by their feelings of incompetence and lack of success.

▶ **Spelling and handwriting:** These skills need to be taught explicitly. Students must achieve a level of automaticity in both.

Developing clear and accurate expression through writing presents major problems for most students with learning difficulties. Written language is perhaps the most difficult of all skills to acquire because its development involves the effective coordination of many different cognitive, linguistic and psycho-motor processes. Sturm and Koppenhaver (2000) tell us that composing for writing involves complex thinking that must integrate multiple components including the topic or theme, choice of words, organisation, purpose, audience, clarity, sequence, cohesion and transcription. Competence in writing in different genres and for different purposes relies heavily on possession of adequate vocabulary, knowledge of syntactical structures, and appropriate strategies for planning, composing, reviewing and revising written language. The ability to generate ideas and organise appropriate content for writing also needs some measure of creativity and imagination (Rief, 2006). Writers also need to be able to spell the necessary words with some accuracy; and finally, writing requires fine-motor coordination and automaticity in handwriting or keyboarding.

It is because writing is a complex skill involving multiple processes and abilities that problems can arise for some students. There is reason to suppose that the number of students with writing difficulties is even greater than the number experiencing difficulties in reading with understanding (Lindstrom, 2007). Saddler et al. (2004, p. 3) wisely remark that, 'Good writing is not only hard work, it is an extremely complex and challenging mental task'.

The National Commission on Writing (2003) considers that writing is the neglected 'R' within the 3Rs. In Australian schools, for example, the OECD (2007) reports that less time is spent teaching writing than in any other developed country. There has also been much less international research focused on effective ways of teaching and improving writing compared to the amount of research on reading and mathematics. It is only in recent years that investigation of methods for helping students improve their writing has gained momentum. The National Commission (2003, p. 51) states:

> Developing fluency in writing has been a fundamental aim of education, even if the promise has never been fully realized. In today's complex, high technology world, the importance of writing as a fundamental organizing objective of education is no less valid or practical. Writing, properly understood, is thought on paper. Increasingly, in the information age, it is also thought on screen, a richly elaborated, logically connected amalgam of ideas, words, themes, images and multimedia designs.

The simple view of writing

Just as the key components of reading ability have been condensed into a simple but functional model (see Chapter 2), writing ability has also been interpreted in the same way by Berninger et al. (2002). Their simple view of writing considers that the active creation of text involves on the one hand lower-order transcription skills such as handwriting, punctuation and spelling, and on the other hand, higher-order self-regulated thinking processes involved in planning, sequencing and expressing the content. The more automatic the lower-order skills become the more that working-memory capacity is available for thinking, composing and revising.

The advantage of this simple model is that it highlights the need to use teaching strategies and activities that ensure all lower-order transcription skills are thoroughly taught and practised until they can be performed with a high degree of automaticity. It also signals the need to instruct students explicitly in the use of effective cognitive strategies for planning, composing and revising text. Saddler (2006) confirms that poor writers typically exhibit major difficulties at two levels, namely coping with grammar, spelling, punctuation and handwriting (lower level), and generating ideas, sequencing the content and revising (higher level).

Studies over the past decade have yielded evidence that explicit instruction in these areas does bring about improvement in students' writing, and in their motivation and confidence as writers (e.g., Chalk et al., 2005; Collins, 1998; De La Paz, 2007; Graham & Harris, 2005; Isaacson, 2004). The benefit is often seen to be greatest (the effect size can be as high as 1.02)[1] when explicit strategy training is used with the weakest writers (Graham & Perin, 2007a; Saddler et al., 2004; Schumaker & Deshler, 2003). Some of these strategies for writing are described in Chapter 6.

Proficient and less proficient writers

Competent writers have not only mastered mechanical aspects of writing but also have a sound understanding of the structure and style of expression needed for different purposes in writing (Lin et al., 2007; Vanderburg, 2006). Proficient writers display a much deeper awareness of all aspects

---

1 Effect size is a statistical measure of the strength of an intervention. Effect size of less than 0.3 suggests little or no effect, 0.3–0.5 a small positive effect, 0.5–0.8 a moderate effect. Above 0.9 is a powerful effect.

of the writing process – generating ideas, planning scope and sequence, drafting and revising. They use well-honed methods for organising their material and presenting their ideas in a clear, detailed and interesting manner to engage their audience (Saddler & Graham, 2007). Most good writers are self-motivated and will engage willingly in writing for its intrinsic rewards. By engaging often in writing they continue to build their skills and strategies through successful practice and with feedback from others.

Less competent writers display none of these traits and abilities. They find the task of writing very difficult and unrewarding, and their lack of skill results in minimal work output. Over time, they engage in much less practice in writing than their more competent peers, and through ongoing lack of practice they do not improve.

Motivation and anxiety problems often accompany the process of writing for those who are not proficient, and can seriously interfere with the quality and quantity of text the student produces (Lindstrom, 2007). The attitude of weak writers toward writing becomes entirely negative ('I can't write, so I hate writing') and they avoid the task whenever possible. A self-perpetuating failure cycle is quickly established. Weak writers' perceptions of their own lack of competence adversely affect their willingness to engage in and persevere with writing tasks (Wilson & Trainin, 2007). Their principal areas of weakness are described more fully below. Fortunately, numerous studies have demonstrated that poor writers can be helped to improve very significantly by teaching them the types of planning, revising and other self-regulatory strategies that are employed by more skilful writers (Graham & Harris, 2003).

The challenge for teachers is to restore students' lost interest and motivation for writing. A classroom where the atmosphere encourages all students to experiment with writing and to take risks without fear of criticism is a necessary but insufficient condition to achieve this change. Weaker writers will still need a very large amount of support and guidance from their teachers to reach the stage where they can recognise their own progress. For some students it may be necessary at first to use various incentives and rewards (extrinsic motivation) to increase the time they spend engaged in writing. It is also necessary to ensure that students attempt to write about topics that genuinely interest them and to which they can relate at a personal level. Some of the activities recommended in the next chapter may help these students gain some measure of increased success and thus restore a degree of confidence.

Evidence indicates that in general male students have more difficulty than female students in acquiring mastery of writing (Hansen, 2002; UKLA/PNS, 2004). Boys therefore need particular attention from teachers in terms of selecting the most relevant and motivating themes for writing, and in the amount of guidance and positive feedback they receive (see the Links box at the end of the chapter).

Areas of difficulty

In order to plan and implement support for struggling writers, it is necessary first to identify their areas of specific difficulty. The research work of Graves (1983) emphasised the value of viewing students' written work diagnostically to determine where each one is located on a developmental continuum from beginning writer to proficient writer. It is also necessary to observe the strategies a student is already using, and what he or she can do unaided. Romeo (2008) strongly supports the view that students' daily writing should be used in a formative assessment manner by teachers to determine their students' strengths and identify what still needs to be taught.

Research studies investigating the characteristics of weaker writers have suggested that the principal areas of concern are those listed below.

> *Weak writers produce a much smaller amount of work than more proficient writers*

To break into the cycle of negativity and avoidance, it is necessary to find ways of simplifying writing tasks to make them more achievable for weaker writers (Saddler, 2006). Examples of this may include talking through key aspects of what is to be written before the students begin to work; providing key words, phrases and opening sentences on the whiteboard; using gapped paragraphs in which the student only needs to add material; teaching the student a strategy for expanding upon basic ideas. It should also be noted that using a word processor for writing often results in students working much harder and producing longer written texts (Polkinghorne, 2004).

> *Weak writers spend little or no time thinking and planning before they start to write*

Lack of planning is one of the reasons why some students write very little, and why their ideas are not presented in a logical order or with sufficient detail (Hess & Wheldall, 1999; Saddler & Graham, 2007). Saddler (2006) indicates that the content of their writing is less coherent than that of proficient writers, and is lacking necessary elaboration of main points. Effective writing requires the writer to spend adequate time generating ideas and sequencing these ideas into the best order before starting to write. This process does not seem to come naturally to weaker writers, so they need to be taken through the planning stage in a more structured manner with the teacher clearly modelling the steps. Teaching students to use a 'story planner' strategy can also be of great help (see Chapter 6). As with all strategy training, the process will need to be repeated many times, with frequent reminders of its purpose and value.

> *Weak writers are usually reluctant to review, edit and polish a first draft*

The 'process approach' to writing (Graves, 1983) helps young writers understand that a first attempt at writing rarely produces a high-quality finished product. Effective writing usually has to pass through a number of stages, starting with the initial formulation of ideas through to the first written draft, with subsequent editing and revising to yield the final product (Hess & Wheldall, 1999; Saddler & Graham, 2007). This planning, composing, editing and publishing sequence must be made clear to students, and they must have many opportunities to go through the stages with feedback.

In the process approach, students confer with the teacher and with their peers to obtain comments and suggestions on their written work as it progresses. Wojasinski and Smith (2002) acknowledge that students with learning difficulties are often resistant to going through the stages of process writing, preferring instead to write quickly to get the job done. However, they also report that when weak writers are actively taken through the stages with plenty of encouragement from the teacher their results are always better.

> *Weaker writers tend to be preoccupied with the mechanical aspects of writing*

This has been identified as one of the main characteristics of students with a specific learning disability in writing (Connelly et al., 2006); but it is also a common problem with almost all weak writers too (Graham & Harris, 2005; Lin et al., 2007). While transcription skills are reasonably important, they are certainly not as important as the creation and expression of good ideas during the composing stage of the task. The tendency to obsess over lower-order skills may reflect the undue importance that parents (and some teachers) attach to accuracy and neatness whenever a student writes. It may also occur because a student lacks automaticity in handwriting or keyboarding, and the transcription process is therefore laboured. It is reported that some 23 per cent of students have significant difficulties with handwriting (Graham et al., 2008) and that poor handwriting and spelling interfere with the composition process by draining too much cognitive effort away from the creative and expressive components. Cognitive load increases significantly for writers when they must consciously attend to the mechanical sub-processes of writing (Christensen, 2005).

> *Weaker writers have problems with spelling*

Learning to spell in a language like English is not an easy task, and many students have difficulties generating the correct spelling of the words they want to use in their writing (Saddler, 2006; Thomson & Snow, 2002). In the past two decades their problem has been compounded by the trend in schools to devote very little time to formal instruction in spelling. Instead, from the early years of schooling, children have been encouraged to invent their own spelling so that they can concentrate more on content and on writing interesting text. The whole language approach and process writing have encouraged teachers to deal with spelling at an individual level, as part of the corrective feedback given to students on their written work. More recently, this perspective has been challenged and it is now believed that spelling skills should be explicitly taught as part of instruction in using the alphabetic code (e.g., Edwards, 2003; Fresch, 2007; Medwell & Wray, 2007; Thomson & Snow, 2002). Learning to spell, like learning to read, is not a natural language process so students need instruction that equips them with effective strategies for analysing and encoding words. Spelling difficulties are present not only in students who exhibit general problems in writing but also in some students who are otherwise very good readers and writers. For this reason it is worth looking at spelling difficulty in more detail.

Proficient and less proficient spellers

Individuals who are confident and competent spellers appear to have developed (or have been taught) strategies for analysing the sequence of phonemes in spoken words, for applying grapho-phonic knowledge, and for storing commonly occurring letter patterns in visual and motor memory. They use both phonetic and visual information in flexible and integrated ways and they draw upon their knowledge of word meanings to help spell words they want to use (Dahl et al., 2003; Moats, 1995). Proficient spellers are also skilled in using appropriate resources (e.g., dictionaries, vocabulary lists, computer spell-checkers) to check the spelling of specific words when necessary. When they write, they are willing to take risks – rather than using a simple word in place of a more complex word, they will attempt the more difficult word and check it later. It must be pointed out that proficient spellers are not always *careful* spellers; sometimes their ideas and the speed with which they want to record them take precedence over accuracy. Good spellers may still need to be taught effective strategies for checking and proofreading their own work.

Less proficient spellers have weaknesses in many areas, including word analysis, visual memory, vocabulary knowledge and strategy use. They identify themselves as poor spellers and they lack confidence. When writing, they often limit the range of words they use to those that they can spell. Most students with learning difficulties progress to a phonetic stage of spelling but appear unable to move easily to the application of visual imagery and analogy that would enable them to spell irregular words correctly (Templeton, 2003). In general, they seem unaware of suitable strategies for attempting to learn new words, relying instead on rote memorisation through repetition.

Specific difficulties with spelling

Specific difficulties in spelling appear to stem from weaknesses in three main areas – phonology and phonic skills, visual memory, and the use of spelling strategies.

> *Phonological and phonic skills*

Spelling the majority of unfamiliar words requires the application of phonic knowledge (Jongejan et al., 2007). While it is true that not all words in the English language follow a simple sound-to-letter relationship, there is sufficient phonological information contained within almost all words to give some clue to their possible spelling. Attending to sounds within a word is certainly the starting point for spelling. It is often found that students with spelling difficulties lack phonological awareness and are weak at segmenting words into component sounds and syllables (Moats, 1995). Coupled with this is an inability to connect the sounds accurately to the correct groups of letters that can represent them. Robinson (2001, p. 205) says that, 'For many children, the complex and confusing relation-ship between letter patterns and sounds in English may not be properly learnt unless specific teaching of these patterns is provided'. There is evidence to indicate that specific training in phonemic awareness, coupled with explicit teaching of phonics, has a positive impact on spelling (e.g., Ball & Blachman, 1991). This is not to suggest that the key to excellent spelling is phonics alone, because other strategies such as visual imagery are also essential for dealing with irregular words.

> *Visual memory*

Even when students do manage to reach a phonetic stage in spelling they appear unable to move beyond it because they do not use effective visual strategies to help store images of words and syllables in their visual memory, or to judge whether a word looks correct or incorrect after they have written it. The well-known 'Look-Say-Cover-Write-Check' method for learning to spell irregular words is one example of activating visual imagery to help store important words in memory (Fisher et al., 2007) (see Chapter 6).

> *Spelling strategies*

A major weakness in poor spellers is their adoption of inefficient methods of learning new words or for checking the spelling of words they have written (Darch et al., 2000). They tend to approach spelling as a rote-learning task, giving attention to mastery of one word at a time but not recognising common orthographic units that are shared by many words. Proficient spellers, on the other hand, usually employ a range of flexible strategies to compare and contrast words, and they call upon their knowledge of typical word structure in order to write and check the words they want to use (Williams & Phillips-Birdsong, 2006). Good spellers are strategic in their approach, and Thomson and Snow (2002) recommend increased attention to the teaching of effective spelling strategies. Chapter 6 provides specific suggestions for this purpose.

There is wide agreement that instruction in spelling for students with learning difficulties, while linked closely with writing for authentic purposes, needs to be intense, direct, systematic and regular (Graham, 2000; Graham & Harris, 1994). It must also be instruction that promotes better knowledge of the spelling system and how it operates. Unfortunately, the evidence suggests that teachers in general are not very effective in exposing students to a range of spelling strategies (possibly because they are not aware of them), encouraging instead mainly rote memorisation methods (Fresch, 2007; Johnston, 2001). In major part this must be due to lack of professional training in the teaching of spelling.

Automaticity in spelling

Spelling, particularly of common everyday words, is a skill that needs to become automatic. Lack of automaticity seriously hampers the ability of students to express their ideas clearly and easily in writing. Correct spelling only becomes automatic if students have regular and intensive periods in which to write, and if they receive support and corrective feedback from the teacher and peers.

Medwell and Wray (2007) and Christensen (2005) suggest that the automatic spelling skill that develops through practice is dependent upon what they term efficient 'orthographic-motor integration' – meaning that competent spellers internalise common letter sequences (orthographic units) as a *physical* response expressed through the fingers as they write. These units, once internalised, then flow automatically from the pen (or through the keyboard) as proficient writers produce their work. In many ways this psycho-motor mastery of orthographic units in writing parallels what occurs with rapid word recognition in reading; thus instant recognition and recall of specific groups of letters underpins both reading and spelling. Shahar-Yames and Share (2008) suggest that the process of spelling may actually facilitate the acquisition of both phonic and visual skills because it requires close attention to letter sequences.

Medwell and Wray (2007) point out that to facilitate effective orthographic-motor integration, young children should be taught to develop a smooth and efficient writing style. Many years before, Peters (1974) had also identified the connection between a swift and easy handwriting style and spelling ability.

Handwriting difficulties

Handwriting is a potent influence on both writing and spelling. Helping students develop a comfortable style of writing from an early age should be regarded as an important goal in all schools (Edwards, 2003; Graham et al., 2000; Medwell & Wray, 2008). Graham et al. (2005) have observed that explicit instruction in handwriting and spelling improves not only those skills but also leads to improved quality and quantity of written work. Unfortunately, such teaching rarely happens now in schools because less than 20 per cent of trainee teachers receive any instruction at all in how to teach handwriting (Graham et al., 2008); and handwriting as a topic has all but faded from most primary school curricula. Medwell and Wray (2007) remark that whole language approach and process writing tended to shift attention away from handwriting, leaving children to acquire it almost incidentally.

It is never too late to help students develop an easier style of handwriting, and there is evidence that in doing so their writing improves in length and quality (Christensen, 2005). Handwriting can only become swift and automatic if students frequently engage in writing, are motivated to do so, and receive relevant corrective feedback.

Dysgraphia

Dysgraphia is the pseudo-clinical term used to describe a specific disability in writing that is more severe, and more resistant to remediation, than the general difficulties encountered by other weak writers (Cavey, 2000). The *Diagnostic and statistical manual of mental disorders* (DSM-IV: APA, 2000) refers to dysgraphia as a 'disorder of written expression'. The prevalence of a serious writing difficulty of this type is not high – possibly much less than 8 per cent of the population (Lindstrom, 2007).

Dysgraphia is believed to be due primarily to neurological causes rather than to lack of teaching or practice. The term is sometimes used to describe illegible handwriting, but it actually covers all problems with written language, including clarity, accuracy and spelling. Dysgraphia is a frequent accompaniment to dyslexia (Berninger et al., 2008); and some symptoms of dysgraphia are often seen in students with attention deficit hyperactivity disorder (ADHD) (Barkley, 2003).

There are no 'special' or alternative methods for use with dysgraphic students. Teaching approaches that are designed to help all weaker writers improve are equally applicable for use with these students. Even those with the most severe writing problems can be helped to improve through direct teaching and opportunities to write each day with constructive and corrective feedback from teacher and peers.

Dysorthographia

A specific disability affecting spelling is referred to as dysorthographia. It is sometimes said that the spelling errors made by dysorthographic students are qualitatively different from those made by other students with weak spelling. Their errors are often referred to as 'bizarre' in that there is little or no connection between the letters they write and the phonemes occurring within the word (Thomson, 1995). It is argued that their problem stems from lack of ability in segmenting spoken words into separate sounds.

Dysorthographic students also appear to be particularly insensitive to the way in which clusters of letters representing pronounceable sub-units within words occur consistently across a number of different words. This results in an inability to develop automaticity in spelling.

The following chapter provides practical advice on methods for addressing some of the difficulties identified in this chapter.

LINKS TO MORE ON WRITING AND SPELLING

▶ A useful overview of writing difficulties is available on the website of the Public Broadcasting Service (PBS). The material relates to a documentary program *Misunderstood minds*. Available online at: http://www.pbs.org/wgbh/misunderstoodminds/writingbasics.html and at http://www.pbs.org/wgbh/misunderstoodminds/writingdiffs.html

▶ For information on the National Writing Project in the US that began in 1974 and still continues, visit http://www.nwp.org/ This site also links to some useful resources for teaching writing.

▶ The report *Writing and school reform* (National Commission on Writing, 2006) together with *The neglected 'R': The need for a writing revolution*, can be located online at: http://www.writingcommission.org/prod_downloads/writingcom/writing-school-reform-natl-comm-writing.pdf

▶ DfES (Department of Education and Skills) (2005) *Raising standards in writing: Achieving children's targets*. Available online at: http://www.standards.dfes.gov.uk/primary/publications/literacy/1160811/

▶ UKLA/ PNS (United Kingdom Literacy Association/ Primary National Strategy) (2004) *Raising boys' achievements in writing*, Royston, Hertfordshire: UKLA. Available online at: http://www.standards.dfes.gov.uk/primary/publications/literacy/1094843/pns_ukla_boys094304report.pdf

Improving writing and spelling

▶ **Learning to write:** Writing is a complex and demanding skill. If students are to become confident and competent writers, they require explicit instruction and many opportunities to write.

▶ **Strategies for writing:** Research evidence strongly supports the view that students benefit from instruction in specific strategies for writing. Struggling writers don't necessarily lack ability or imagination they simply lack effective strategies for planning, composing and refining their text.

▶ **Spelling:** Spelling can be improved by effective instruction that combines direct teaching of spelling principles and appropriate strategies for learning new words.

The National Commission on Writing (2006) has stressed the need for schools to devote more time each day to activities that require students to engage in meaningful writing. Indeed, the Commission recommends *doubling* the amount of time that is typically spent at the moment. It is also felt that in some classrooms the development of writing skills is left too much to incidental learning and informal methods.

There are so many different challenges involved in becoming a proficient writer that students need explicit guidance and support. All students benefit from specific instruction in the writing process and in the use of effective strategies for planning, monitoring, evaluating and editing their written work. In order to develop students' motivation, skills and strategies for writing, teachers need to use both direct instruction (demonstrations, modelling, 'thinking aloud', guided practice) and indirect instruction (constructive feedback).

Teaching students to write

Traditionally there have been two main approaches to teaching writing – a skills-based approach and, more recently, the 'process' approach (Pollington et al., 2001). A skills-based approach involves a fairly structured program with direct teaching of essential skills and concepts. Students' writing ability is developed through topics selected mainly by the teacher or set within a textbook. Students also engage in practice exercises covering aspects of grammar, sentence construction, spelling and punctuation. The major criticisms of a skills-based approach are that it usually fails to motivate students, and it does not encourage independence in writing. It is believed that learning to write is more motivating and authentic when students have the opportunity to write freely on topics they have chosen for themselves or that have emerged naturally from subjects or themes studied in the classroom.

The process approach to writing emerged in the 1980s, with a shift of emphasis from skills-based instruction to a more student-centred approach (Graves, 1983). Process writing is typically implemented through various models such as 'writers' workshops', 'shared writing', 'guided writing' and the 'conference approach'. The focus in these models is on engaging students in interesting and motivating writing for real purposes, rather than teaching writing skills through contrived exercises. The actual process of writing is made explicit to students, starting with the planning and gathering of ideas, through the various stages of drafting and revising to the final finished product. Students are able to see that any piece of writing does not have to be perfect from the start but can be polished and improved many times. Writers are guided and supported as they move through the complete process of drafting, editing and publishing.

Writers' Workshop in primary school provides a good example of the process approach. It involves a whole-class writing session in which all students are engaged in various writing activities and are supported in their endeavours by their classmates and teacher. The topic or theme for the writing may come from the teacher, but is more likely to be chosen by the students. It is believed that selecting a personal topic rather than a teacher-set topic is not only more motivating but reduces the cognitive load involved in planning and generating ideas for a less familiar theme. As each student's writing develops during the lesson, a partner can read each draft and make constructive suggestions. Group sharing and peer editing are essential elements in writers' workshop; so too is collaborative writing – two students working together to produce a story or report, sometimes referred to as 'paired writing'. Graham and Perin (2007a) suggest that collaborative writing as a teaching and learning approach produces an effect size of about 0.75, indicating that it is an effective method for raising achievement.

As far as possible, the teacher should also confer with every student, encouraging the writer to reflect upon clarity, accuracy, interest and relevance of the text. Specific writing skills can be taught at the same time through this individualised approach. Differences in ability among the students in the class will determine the amount of time the teacher needs to spend with individuals. Mini lessons may also be provided for the whole class if the teacher identifies a common problem or misunderstanding, or if a particular teaching point needs to be made.

Shared writing and guided writing sessions embody basically the same principles as those applied in writers' workshop (Fountas & Pinnell, 2001; Oczkus, 2007; Worthy et al., 2001). However, guided writing usually entails more direct modelling by the teacher of specific writing strategies, styles and genres, followed by guided and independent application of the same strategies by the students. A teacher could begin, for example, by demonstrating at the whiteboard how to generate ideas for a given topic, how to create and organise an opening paragraph, and how to develop the remaining ideas in logical sequence. Students then take it in turns to present their own material to the group, receiving constructive feedback from peers. The guided approach is generally believed to be more effective than either the traditional teacher-directed method, or the unstructured use of process method, in fostering writing skills (Graham & Perin, 2007b).

As an element of the guidance aspect, Fountas and Pinnell (2001) recommend providing writers with guidelines to help them self-evaluate and revise their written work. For example, the guidelines might ask:

▶ Did you begin with an interesting sentence?
▶ Are your ideas easy to understand?
▶ Are your ideas presented in the best sequence?
▶ Did you give examples to help readers understand your points?
▶ Is your writing interesting?
▶ Have you used paragraphs?
▶ Have you checked spelling and punctuation?

The way in which self-regulatory strategies of this type have been introduced into process approaches to writing reflects, perhaps, a slight swing back toward more structured teaching (Argys, 2008). Instruction in effective strategies for writing has certainly been a positive step, and represents a sound balance between skills-based and process methods (Graham & Perin, 2007a).

Applying a strategic approach to writing

In the same way that strategy training has been used effectively to improve reading comprehension, strategy training can also be very effective in improving students' writing. A number of studies have shown that teaching students to apply appropriate plans of action results in marked improvement in the quality of their written products (Collins, 1998; De La Paz, 2007; Harris et al., 2002; Saddler et al., 2004). Chalk et al. (2005) report that students begin to exhibit more sophisticated writing once they develop effective strategies for planning or revising text, and as they learn to self-regulate.

Strategy training typically involves teaching students to follow a sequence of steps as they make their way through the various stages of planning, transcribing, evaluating and improving their writing on a chosen topic.

Emphasis is placed on metacognitive aspects of the writing process (e.g. thinking, checking for clarity, self-monitoring, self-correction). Often the steps are summarised in the form of an acronym or mnemonic to aid recall. Examples of this are provided later. A strategy is often presented as a set of questions that writers need to ask themselves to facilitate the generation of ideas and to assist with the organisation of their material across different writing genres.

In the early stages of learning new strategies students may be required to verbalise the questions as they work through the plan of action. When they become more confident in using the strategy independently such verbalising is unnecessary. Saddler et al. (2004) suggest the use of a 'think sheet' to help students respond to the steps in a strategy. Each student is given a sheet that summarises the strategy and writes notes and ideas in response to each prompt – such as 'Who are the characters in your story?' 'Where does this take place?' (see the Links box at the end of the chapter).

It is always necessary to continue strategy training and practice beyond the point where students first seem to grasp the idea and apply it. Mastery and independent use of a strategy will only come after considerable overlearning (Graham & Harris, 2005). The steps in a strategy can be summarised and displayed permanently as a self-help poster on the classroom wall. They can also be duplicated in note form for each student to retain in the back of his or her exercise book for reference.

Isaacson (2004) states that explicit instruction in writing strategies must involve the teacher in giving clear demonstrations, explanations and modelling, followed by guided practice with feedback, leading eventually to students' independent use. Isaacson also suggests that, when demonstrating, teachers need to highlight critical features of different forms of text (e.g. narrative, factual report, verse, etc.) so that students become more versatile in text construction for different purposes.

When discussing their Self Regulated Strategy Development model (SRSD) – a structured approach for planning, drafting and revising text – Graham and Perin (2007b) recommend a specific teaching sequence. Under SRSD students are also taught to set themselves goals, to self-monitor, reflect, and correct or revise their texts as appropriate. The recommended teaching process involves the following steps:

▶ Describe and discuss the value of the strategy.

▶ Model the strategy through clear demonstration and thinking aloud.

▶ Ask students to memorise the steps involved.

▶ Support and guide students' initial applications of the strategy.

▶ Aim for independent use by students.

Schumaker and Deshler (2003) reviewed the research evidence on using a strategic approach to writing with students with learning difficulties. The strategies they examined covered sentence construction, paragraph writing, planning, composing, error monitoring and self-correction. They concluded that strategies that can be *easily applied and remembered* are powerful in improving the writing of these students. Graham and Perin (2007a) and Saddler (2006) confirm this conclusion, reporting that the explicit teaching of strategies typically produces an effect size above 1.02 for students with learning difficulties, indicating a very strong positive influence on students' ability to write more effectively.

Obstacles to strategy training

Despite the benefits of strategy training for almost all students, there are still a few individuals who do not seem to make effective use of the writing strategies they have been taught. Vanderburg (2006) suggests that this may occur for four possible reasons:

▶ They do not find the strategy useful.

▶ They know it is useful but still do not remember to use it.

▶ They don't use it because it places too heavy a demand on their already overstretched cognitive resources.

▶ Not enough time is devoted to writing, so the strategy is not practised and reinforced sufficiently.

De La Paz (2007) suggests that some strategies are unnecessarily complex, with too many steps to remember and implement. Although potentially effective, these strategies would be much easier to recall and use if simplified.

The greatest problem with strategy training is that students tend not to generalise the use of the strategy to writing situations outside the context in which it is first taught. Graham and Harris (2005) suggest that better generalisation and transfer may be achieved by:

▷ helping students understand how a strategy works, and how it helps them produce better results

▷ leading students to consider when and where a particular strategy can be used

▷ discussing how to modify a strategy for different situations

▷ teaching students to use self statements as a means to reinforce strategy use.

Examples of strategies for writing

Although there are many different writing strategies referred to in the literature, they all tend to have common aims and characteristics. They all focus on helping students think productively before writing, and then to sequence their ideas logically, add relevant detail, impose structure on their text, and then review and improve their first draft. The following examples will serve as typical illustrations of specific strategies for writing.

> *POW and TREE*

This is a two-part strategy to help students write opinion essays. The authors report that this strategy can be effective with students with learning difficulties, and can even be used as early as Grade 3 (Harris et al., 2002). The students are taught to apply the following step-by-step procedure:

P = Pick your topic or idea.

O = Organise your thoughts and make notes.

W = Write, and then say more.

T = Topic sentence – state your opinion.

R = Give at least three reasons to support that belief.

E = Explain your reasons in more detail.

E = End with a good concluding statement.

> *POW and WWW + What 2 + How 2*

This strategy is for narrative story writing (Saddler, 2006). POW is explained above.

WWW stands for:

(a) **W**ho are the characters? (b) **W**hen does the story take place? (c) **W**here does the story take place?

What 2 represents:

(a) *What* do the characters do? (b) *What* happens?

How 2 reminds the writer to:

(a) State *how* the story ends. (b) *How* did the characters feel?

This strategy has been used successfully with Grade 2 students who were taught for 30 minutes sessions three times per week (total of 11 lessons). Saddler (2006) reports that the students wrote longer stories of better quality, because they gave more thought to planning. POW plus WWW + What 2 + How 2 contains far too many steps for students to remember unaided, so it needs to be supported by use of a cue card or prompt sheet.

> PLAN and WRITE

These researchers taught students the mnemonics PLAN (to be used at the planning stage of writing), and WRITE (to be used at the composing and transcription stages)(Graham & Perin, 2007b).

P = Pay attention to topic. Set your goals.
L = List your main ideas.
A = Add supporting detail.
N = Number the ideas in sequence.
W = Work from your plan.
R = Remember the goals
I = Include transition words to move from one paragraph to the next.
T = Try different kinds of sentences.
E = Exciting and interesting content.

> Story planner

Using a story planner is also effective for helping students brainstorm ideas before narrative writing, and arranging the ideas in the best sequence (Westwood, 2007). The story planner can take the form of a graphic organiser that provides a starting point for generating ideas. The topic title is written in a circle in the centre of the whiteboard. From this circle a number of 'spokes' branch out like rays from the sun. As ideas related to the title are suggested, each one is added to one of the spokes until a suitable quantity of ideas have been recorded. Prompts and cues can be used to stimulate students' thinking. Ideas might include the setting for the story, the type of action to take place, the characters involved, the outcome, etc. As a class, students then review the ideas and decide upon an appropriate starting point for the story. Number '1' is written against that idea. How will the story develop? Students determine the order in which the other ideas will be used, and appropriate numbers are written against each spoke. Some of the ideas may not be used at all and can be erased. Other ideas may need to be added at this stage, and numbered accordingly. Students now use the bank of ideas recorded on the story planner to start writing their own stories. Brief notes can be elaborated into sentences and the sentences gradually extended into paragraphs. By preparing the draft ideas and then discussing the best order in which to write them, students have tackled two of the most difficult problems they face when composing, namely planning and sequencing.

> LESSER (LESSER helps me write more)

Many struggling writers produce very little material during times set aside for writing. This strategy is designed to increase the amount of material these students complete in a lesson, thereby increasing the amount of successful practice (Westwood, 2007).

L = List your ideas.
E = Examine your list.
S = Select your starting point.
S = Sentence one tells us about this first idea.
E = Expand on this first idea with another sentence.
R = Read what you have written. Revise if necessary. Repeat for the next paragraph.

In addition, Stotz et al. (2008) reported that encouraging primary school students with writing difficulties to count and record on a graph the number of words they write each lesson can improve both the quantity and quality of their written work. This strategy for self-monitoring is a key feature of the method known as precision teaching, designed to increase performance (for details, see Westwood, 2008). Many online links to additional examples of writing strategies can be found at the end of this chapter.

The role of technology in supporting writing

Word processors have made the task of writing less daunting for struggling writers. Unlike traditional pen-and-paper writing where changes often necessitate starting again and rewriting large amounts of material, with a computer the text can be easily added to, modified, deleted or moved, and spelling accuracy can be monitored. These changes have improved weak writers' attitude and motivation (Barbetta & Spears-Bunton, 2007; Graham & Perin, 2007a; MacArthur, 2000).

Word processing seems to be of particular benefit to students who don't usually write very much, and to those with the most severe spelling problems. In particular, students with learning difficulties gain confidence in creating, editing, erasing and publishing their own material through a medium that holds their attention and is not critical of their efforts (Hetzroni & Shrieber, 2004). For students with learning difficulties, word processing de-emphasises the mechanical aspects of the task and allows more mental effort to be devoted to generating ideas.

Phillips (2004) identified several advantages in using word processors to encourage students in their writing. The advantages included:

- Mistakes can be corrected without a mess.
- Revisions are made more easily.
- When printed, the finished product looks very professional.
- Students can work collaboratively in the composing and revising stages.
- Finished products can be shared and critiqued easily within the peer group.

In addition to word processing, technology offers a range of programs to enhance writing and spelling. There are programs that provide graphics such as concept maps or 'word webs' (similar to the story planner referred to above) to facilitate brainstorming and pre-writing planning and organisation (Barbetta & Spears-Bunton, 2007). *Write:OutLoud* is a word processing program that can read back to the writer what he or she has written. *Co:Writer* is a word prediction program that offers the writer optional spellings for a word that fits the semantic and syntactical context of a sentence.[1] This program also offers speech output and can read a word when highlighted by the cursor. Heinsch (2001) reports favourably on both programs when used with teenage students with learning difficulties, indicating that their attitude, behaviour and quality of written work all improved.

It is beyond the scope of this book to go into technology and writing in greater depth.

Spelling

As stated in the previous chapter, learning to spell accurately in English is not easy. Some students with perfectly adequate reading and writing abilities still have difficulty spelling some of the words they want to use. In Chapter 5 the disability known as dysorthographia was discussed, but this disability only accounts for a very tiny percentage of individuals with poor spelling. There are many other reasons to account for weakness in spelling, including lack of instruction in spelling principles and a lack of effective ways of learning and recalling words. While dysorthographic students are remarkably resistant to remedial intervention, this is not the case with other weak spellers, and they can make significant improvements if taught correctly.

The instructional aim in spelling is not to teach separately each and every word a person is ever likely to need; this would be an impossible task. The aim is to teach students *how to learn new words* and how to *check and self-correct* their own spelling. The only corpus of words that teachers should insist students master are the hundred or so words that occur most frequently in all forms of writing. In many ways, this list corresponds fairly closely with the basic sight vocabulary lists that exist for reading, and these

---

1   *Write:OutLoud* and *Co:Writer* are both available from Don Johnston Inc, Volo, Illinois.

lists can be used as source material (see the Links box at the end of the chapter).

The main methods or strategies for learning new words include those that deal with a visual approach, those that stress sounding and blending, others that use word meanings to guide spelling, and some that use a multi-modal or multisensory approach to help reinforce correct spellings. These approaches are not mutually exclusive and often the optimum effect can be achieved by combining two or more methods. The key points of each approach are summarised here.

> *Whole-word visual approach*

This method is effective for mastering irregular words that cannot simply be translated into letter-to-sound correspondences (e.g. *juice, ache, work, cough, choir*). The strategy known as Look-Cover-Write-Check (LCWC) – sometimes modified to Look-*Say*-Cover-Write-Check – is one example of this method. The aim is to strengthen visual imagery and enhance the recognition and recall of letter patterns. Studies have found the method to be effective (e.g., Fisher et al., 2007), but some educators have voiced reservations about its use (e.g., Cooke, 1997; Kelly, 2006). The critics suggest that it relies too much on rote memorisation of letter sequences without, at the same time, encouraging a speller to attend to phonic cues within the word. Cooke (1997) says that LCWC does not make full use of the alphabetic nature of the English writing system, nor the role of phonology in spelling both regular and irregular words. Kelly (2006) believes that at the 'look' stage students should be taught to examine the word more carefully, saying the phonemes or the syllables that make up the word, and mentally comparing the word with other known words. Perhaps the steps should really be 'Look *and think* – cover – write – check'.

Implementation of LCWC involves teaching the student the following steps.

▶ Look very carefully at the word. Try to remember every detail.
▶ Say the word clearly.
▶ Close your eyes and imagine you can see the word projected on a screen.
▶ Open your eyes. Cover the word so that you cannot see it.

- Write the word from memory, pronouncing it quietly as you write.
- Check your spelling of the word with the original. If it is not correct, repeat the process until you can produce the word accurately.

Teachers should check for recall several days later. For some students, tracing over the word with a finger may help with assimilation and retention of the letter sequence. See the Links box at the end of the chapter for additional material on LCWC.

> Phonemic approach

This spelling-by-sound method uses the strategy of breaking a target word into its phonemes and then writing the word using phonic principles. The teaching sequence usually progresses from spelling simple consonant-vowel-consonant words to applying more complex letter groups representing pronounceable parts of words (e.g. *−eed, anti−, dis−, −ure*). Some authorities suggest that at this higher level, learning to spell supports learning to read by focusing closely on orthographic units (Ehri & Rosenthal, 2007; Shahar-Yames & Share, 2008). The phonemic approach is only effective when spellers also use visual memory for common letter sequences to check the accuracy of what they have written – in other words, spelling by sound requires the speller also to check whether the word *looks correct*.

> Morphemic approach

This approach is based on using the meaning of a word, or part of the word, to assist with its spelling. A morpheme is the smallest unit of meaning within a word. A word may comprise one morpheme (e.g. *hygiene* = 1), or more (e.g. *hygienic* = 2, *unhygienic* = 3). The word *hygienic* also illustrates that under the morphemic approach the learner is also taught to apply certain rules when changing a root word (*hygiene* drops the 'e' when 'ic' is added). Direct instructional methods are often employed for a morphemic approach. The program *Spelling through morphographs* (Dixon & Engelmann, 1979) is a good example.

> Spelling by analogy

Students are taught to refer to words they can already spell correctly to help them work out the probable spelling of an unfamiliar word that shares some of the same sound characteristics (Kirkbride & Wright, 2002). For example, knowing how to spell the word *each* helps one to spell *beach*, *peach*, *reach*, *teach*, *teacher* and *teaching*. Using visual checking should indicate to the speller that *teeching* looks wrong.

> *Simultaneous oral spelling*

This approach requires a speller to name the letters (*name*, not sound) in correct sequence several times before and during the writing of the word (Weeks et al., 2002). Five steps are involved.

- Select the word you wish to learn. Ask the teacher to pronounce it clearly.
- Pronounce the word clearly yourself while looking carefully at the word.
- Say each syllable in the word (or break a single-syllable word into onset and rime; e.g. /st/– /arch/).
- Name the letters in the word twice or three times.
- Write the word, naming each letter as you write it. Check it.

> *Old way – new way approach*

This corrective approach takes a student's error as the starting point for change (Lyndon, 1989; Fisher et al., 2007). The student's memory of the incorrect spelling ('old way') of the word is used to activate later an awareness of the 'new' (correct) way of spelling the word.

The following steps and procedures are used to teach this approach:

- Student writes the word with the incorrect spelling.
- Teacher and student agree to call this the 'old way' of spelling that word.
- Teacher shows student a 'new way' (correct way) of spelling the word.
- Attention is drawn to the similarities and differences between the old and the new forms.
- Student writes the word again in the old way.
- Student writes the word in the new way, and states clearly the differences.
- Repeat five such writings of old way – new way, and statement of differences.
- Write the word the new way six times, using different colour pens or in different styles.
- Older students may be asked to write six different sentences using the word in its 'new' form.
- Revise the word or words taught after a two-week interval.

▸ If necessary, repeat this procedure every two weeks until the new response is firmly established.

> *Multisensory approach*

This method involves finger tracing over a written version of a target word while looking at it and saying it clearly. The approach is used mainly with students with major learning difficulties, but can also be applied with any student to overcome a particular spelling demon. It is a very slow method, but it can help students store an accurate visual and motor image of the word in long-term memory. Using a keyboard to type words on the computer screen is also multisensory in the sense that the process involves both vision and finger movements.

A strategic approach to spelling

For students to become truly independent in their spelling they need to be able to determine for themselves how best to learn a new word or to attempt to spell an unfamiliar word. They need to consider, for example, whether the word can be written accurately simply by translating sounds to letters (phonemic approach), whether it is an irregular word (thus requiring mainly a visual approach), or whether the word is similar to any word they already know (spelling by analogy). They also need to identify any difficult or unpredictable part of the word. The general purpose spelling strategy from Lam and Westwood (2006) embodies most of these points. The students are taught the self–regulating script below.

▸ Do I know this word?
▸ How many syllables can I hear when I say the word?
▸ Do I know any other word that sounds almost the same?
▸ Which letter-groups do I need to write?
▸ Does the word I have written look correct?
▸ No. I'll try again.
▸ Does this look better? Let me check.

The teaching of spelling should not be confined to English lessons. All subject teachers should accept the responsibility of encouraging accurate spelling in their own area of the curriculum. It is valuable if a subject teacher compiles a core vocabulary list for his or her subject and makes this available to all students as a self-help spelling aid for use when written work is undertaken in that subject.

For more details on all aspects of spelling instruction and assessment, see *What teachers need to know about spelling* in this ACER series.

A final word

It can be seen from the issues discussed in this book that becoming fully literate can present problems for some students. However, their problems can be minimised or even eliminated completely if they are recognised and addressed early. Effective instruction, particularly when it builds confidence and independence in learning, will always raise students' achievement levels.

Rowe (2006, p. 4) observes:

Equipping young people to engage productively in the knowledge economy and in society more broadly is fundamental to both individual and national prosperity. This objective depends primarily on the ability to read and write effectively, and the provision of quality teaching and learning by teachers who have acquired, during their pre-service teacher education, and in-service professional learning, evidence-based teaching practices that are shown to be effective in meeting the developmental and learning needs of all children. Our children and their teachers require no less.

LINKS TO MORE ON STRATEGIES FOR WRITING AND SPELLING

▶ Graham, S. & Perin, D. (2007b). *Writing next: Effective strategies to improve the writing of adolescents in middle and high schools.* Washington, DC: Alliance for Excellence in Education. This is an extremely informative and helpful document outlining the strategies that have been proved by research to enhance students' writing abilities. Available online at: http://www.carnegie.org/literacy/pdf/writingnext.pdf

▶ Many useful classroom teaching strategies for improving writing and composing skills can be found online at the Instructional Strategies Online Database: http://edhd.bgsu.edu/isod and at the University of Nebraska-Lincoln website at. http.//www.unl.edu/csi/writing.shtml

▶ Examples of think sheets for guiding the planning stage of writing are available online at: http://literacy.kent.edu/eureka/strategies/think_sheets.pdf

▶ Information on shared writing and guided writing can be found on the National Strategies website (UK): http://www.standards.dfes.gov.uk/primary/publications/literacy/63541/651161/919597

▶ *Improving writing, with particular focus on supporting boys' writing development.* Available online at: http://www.standards.dfes.gov.uk/primaryframework/downloads/PDF/Paper_on_improving_writing.pdf

▶ *Helping students with the writing process.* Available online at: http://literacy.kent.edu/eureka/strategies/help_writing_process.pdf

▶ *Step up to writing.* Useful step-by-step procedures available online at: http://www2.pylusd.k12.ca.us/glk/jlaurich/StepUpToWriting.htm

▶ *Writing strategies.* http://www.gse.buffalo.edu/org/writingstrategies/

▶ *Look-Cover-Write-Check spelling strategy.* Activities and word lists available at: http://www.amblesideprimary.com/ambleweb/lookcover/lookcover.html

▶ *Spelling rules.* Interesting background material for teachers at: http://www2.gsu.edu/~wwwesl/egw/susan.htm

▶ Core spelling lists of most commonly used words, arranged by grade level. Available online at: http://hastings.lexingtonma.org/curriculum/spelling/spelling-words.html

References

Aaron, P. G., Joshi, R. M., Ayotollah, M., Ellsberry, A., Henderson, J., & Lindsey, K. (1999). Decoding and sight-word naming: Are they independent components of word recognition skill? *Reading and Writing, 11*, 89–127.

AATE/ALEA (Australian Association for Teaching English/Australian Literacy Educators' Association). (2001). *Standards for teachers of English language and literacy in Australia* (STELLA). Online document retrieved June 16, 2008 from. http://www.stella.org.au/

ABS (Australian Bureau of Statistics). (2007). *Adult literacy and life skills survey: Summary results, Australia.* Canberra: ABS.

Adams, M. J. (1990). *Beginning to read: Thinking and learning about print.* Cambridge, Mass: MIT Press.

Allington, R. L. (2001). *What really matters for struggling readers?* New York: Longman.

Alm, R. S. (1981). The educational causes of reading difficulties. *Journal of Research and Development in Education, 14, 4,* 41–49.

American Federation of Teachers. (2007). *Where we stand: K–12 literacy.* Washington, DC: AFT.

APA (American Psychiatric Association). (2000). *Diagnostic and statistical manual of mental disorders: Text revised (DSM–IV–TR).* Washington, DC: APA.

Argys, R. (2008). One more thing: Can we teach process writing and a formulaic response? *English Journal, 97, 3,* 97–101.

Ball, E. W., & Blachman, B. A. (1991). Does phonemic awareness training in kindergarten make a difference in early word recognition and developmental spelling? *Reading Research Quarterly, 27,* 49–66.

Barbetta, P. M., & Spears-Bunton, L. A. (2007). Learning to write: Technology for students with disabilities in secondary inclusive classrooms. *English Journal, 96, 4,* 86–93.

Barkley, R. A. (2003). Attention-Deficit Hyperactivity Disorder. In E. J. Mash & R. A. Barkley (Eds.), *Child psychopathology* (2nd ed.) (pp. 75–143). New York: Guilford.

Benke, C. (2000). Talking books. *Australian Journal of Learning Disabilities, 5, 4,* 33–34.

Berninger, V. W., Nielsen, K. H., Abbott, R. D., Wijsman, E., & Raskind, W. (2008). Writing problems in developmental dyslexia: Under-recognised and under-treated. *Journal of School Psychology, 46, 1,* 1–21.

Berninger, V. W., Vaughn, K., Abbot, R. D., Begay, K., Coleman, K., Curtin, G., Hawkins, J. M., & Graham, S. (2002). Teaching spelling and composition alone and together: Implications for the simple view of writing. *Journal of Educational Psychology, 94, 2,* 291–304.

Berninger, V. W., Vermeulen, K., Abbott, R. D., McCutchen, D., Cotton, S., Cude, J., Dorn, S., & Sharon, T. (2003). Comparison of three approaches to supplementary reading instruction for low-achieving second-grade readers. *Language, Speech and Hearing Services in School, 34, 2,* 101–116.

Biancrosa, G., & Snow, C. E. (2006). *Reading next: A vision for action and research in middle and high school literacy* (2nd ed.). Washington, DC: Alliance for Excellent Education.

Blachman, B. A., Ball, E. W., Black, R., & Tangel, D. M. (2000). *Road to the code: A phonological awareness program for young children.* Baltimore, MD: Brookes.

Blanton, W. E., Wood, K. D., & Taylor, D. B. (2007). Rethinking middle school reading instruction: A basic literacy activity. *Reading Psychology, 28,* 75–95.

Boulware-Gooden, R., Carreker, S., Thornhill, A., & Joshi, R. M. (2007). Instruction of metacognitive strategies enhances reading comprehension and vocabulary achievement of third grade students. *Reading Teacher, 61, 1,* 70–77.

Brandt, D., & Clinton, K. (2002). Limits of the local: Explaining perspectives on literacy as a social practice. *Journal of Literacy Research, 34, 3,* 337–356.

Bruce, M., & Robinson, G. (2002). The effectiveness of a metacognitive approach to teaching word identification skills to upper primary poor readers. *Special Education Perspectives, 11, 1,* 3–30.

Burns, E. (2006). Pause, prompt and praise – Peer tutored reading for pupils with learning difficulties. *British Journal of Special Education, 33, 2,* 62–67.

Burns, M., Griffin, P., & Snow, C. (1999). *Starting out right: A guide to promoting children's reading success.* Washington, DC: National Academy Press.

Cain, K., & Oakhill, J. (2006). Profiles of children with specific reading comprehension difficulties. *British Journal of Educational Psychology, 76, 4,* 683–696.

Carver, R. P. (2000). *The causes of high and low reading achievement.* Mahwah, NJ: Erlbaum.

Castles, A., & Nation, K. (2008). Learning to be a good orthographic reader. *Journal of Research in Reading, 31, 1,* 1–7.

Cavey, D. W. (2000). *Dysgraphia: Why Johnny can't write* (3rd ed.). Austin, TX: ProEd.

Center, Y., Freeman, L., & Robertson, G. (1998). An evaluation of the Schoolwide Early Literacy and Language Program (SWELL) in six disadvantaged NSW schools. *International Journal of Disability, Development and Education, 45*, 143–172.

Chalk, J. C., Hagan-Burke, S., & Burke, M. D. (2005). The effects of self-regulated strategy development on the writing process for high school students with learning disabilities. *Learning Disability Quarterly, 28, 1*, 75–87.

Chan, L., & Dally, K. (2002). Review of literature. In W. Louden, et al. (Eds.), *Mapping the territory: Primary students with learning difficulties in literacy and numeracy*, Canberra: Department of Education, Training and Youth Affairs.

Christensen, C. A. (2005). The role of orthographic-motor integration in the production of creative and well-structured written texts for students in secondary school. *Educational Psychology, 25, 5*, 441–453.

Clay, M. M. (1993). *Reading Recovery: A guidebook for teachers in training.* Auckland: Heinemann.

Cohen-Mimran, R., & Sapir, S. (2007). Deficits in working memory in young adults with reading disabilities. *Journal of Communication Disorders, 40, 2*, 168–183.

Coiro, J., & Dobler, E. (2007). Exploring the online reading comprehension strategies used by sixth-grade skilled readers to search for and locate information on the Internet. *Reading Research Quarterly, 42, 2*, 214–257.

Collins, J. L. (1998). *Strategies for struggling writers.* New York. Guilford Press.

Coltheart, M., & Prior, M. (2006). Learning to read in Australia. *Australian Journal of Learning Disabilities, 11, 4*, 157–164.

Commonwealth Department of Education, Science and Training. (2002). *The use of data to inform effective intervention in literacy and numeracy programs in the early years of schooling.* Canberra: DEST.

Connelly, V., Campbell, S., MacLean, M., & Barnes, J. (2006). Contribution of lower order skills to the written composition of college students with and without dyslexia. *Developmental Neuropsychology, 29, 1*, 175–196.

Cooke, A. (1997). Learning to spell difficult words: Why Look, Cover, Write and Check is not enough. *Dyslexia, 3, 4*, 240–243.

Cowey, W. (2007). *Exploring the potential of classroom: Questioning in the National Accelerated Literacy Program.* Paper presented to the Australian Literacy Educators Association Conference, July 2007, Canberra.

Cragg, L., & Nation, K. (2006). Exploring written narrative in children with poor reading comprehension. *Educational Psychology, 26, 1*, 55–72.

Cramer, K., & Rosenfeld, S. (2008). Effect of degree of challenge on reading performance. *Reading and Writing Quarterly, 24, 1*, 119–137.

Crevola, C., & Hill, P. (2005). *The Children's Literacy Success Study (ClaSS): A research report on the first six years of a large-scale reform initiative.* Melbourne: Catholic Education Office.

Cunningham, P., Hall, D., & Sigmon, C. (2001). *Four Blocks Literacy Model.* Greensboro, NC: Carson-Dellosa Publishing. Retrieved February 21, 2008 from: http://www.four-blocks.com/index.htm

Dahl, K., & Associates (2003). Connecting developmental word study with classroom writing: Children's descriptions of spelling strategies. *Reading Teacher, 57, 4*, 310–319.

Darch, C., Kim, S., & Johnson, J. H. (2000). The strategic spelling skills of students with learning disabilities: The results of two studies. *Journal of Instructional Psychology, 27*, 15–26.

Davies, A., & Ritchie, D. (2004). *Teaching Handwriting, Reading and Spelling Skills* (THRASS). Chester: THRASS (UK) Ltd.

DCSF (Department for Children, Schools and Families, UK). (2006). *The new conceptual framework for teaching reading: the 'simple view of reading' – Overview for literacy leaders and managers in schools and early years settings.* Online document from Primary National Strategy, UK. Retrieved June 15, 2008 from: http://www.teachers.gov.uk/docbank/index.cfm?id=11279

De Jong, P. F., & Share, D. L. (2007). Orthographic learning during oral and silent reading. *Scientific Studies of Reading, 11, 1*, 55–71.

De La Paz, S. (2007). Managing cognitive demands of writing: Comparing the effects of instructional components in strategy instruction. *Reading and Writing Quarterly, 23, 3*, 249–266.

De Lemos, M. (2005). Effective strategies for the teaching of reading: What works, and why. *Australian Journal of Learning Disabilities, 10, 3/4*, 11–17.

Department of Education, Employment and Training (Victoria). (2001). *Middle years successful interventions literacy project.* Melbourne: Author.

DEST (Department of Education, Science and Training: Australia). (2005). *Teaching reading: National inquiry into the teaching of literacy.* Canberra: AGPS, Commonwealth of Australia.

Dixon, R., & Engelmann, S. (1979). *Spelling through morphographs.* Chicago, IL: Science Research Associates.

Dodge, B. (1995). WebQuest: A technique for Internet-based learning. *Distance Educator, 1, 2*, 10–13.

Donat, D. J. (2006). 'Reading Their Way': A balanced approach that increases achievement. *Reading and Writing Quarterly, 22*, 305–323.

Donnell, W. J. (2007). The effects of multisensory vowel instruction during word study for third grade students. *Reading Research Quarterly, 42, 4*, 468–471.

Edwards, L. (2003). Writing instruction in kindergarten. *Journal of Learning Disabilities. 36, 2,* 136–148.

Ehri, L. C. (1997). Sight word learning in normal readers and dyslexics. In B. A. Blachman (Ed.), *Foundations of reading acquisition and dyslexia* (pp. 163–198). Mahwah, NJ: Erlbaum.

Ehri, L. C., Dreyer, L. G., Flugman, B., & Gross, A. (2007). Reading Rescue: An effective tutoring intervention model for language minority students who are struggling readers in first grade. *American Educational Research Journal, 44, 2,* 414–448.

Ehri, L. C., Nunes, S. R., Stahl, S. A., & Willows, D. M. (2001a). Systematic phonics instruction helps students learn to read: Evidence from the National Reading Panel's meta-analysis. *Review of Educational Research, 71,* 393–47.

Ehri, L. C., Nunes, S. R., Willows, D. M., Shuster, B. V., Yaghoub-Zadeh, Z., & Shanahan, T. (2001b). Phonemic awareness instruction helps children learn to read: Evidence from the National Reading Panel's meta-analysis. *Reading Research Quarterly, 36,* 250–287.

Ehri, L. C., & Rosenthal, J. (2007). Spellings of words: A neglected facilitator of vocabulary learning. *Journal of Literacy Research, 39, 4,* 389–409.

Eldredge, J. L. (2005). *Teach decoding: Why and how* (2nd ed.). Upper Saddle River, NJ: Pearson-Merrill-Prentice Hall.

Ellis, L. A. (2005). *Balancing approaches: Revisiting the educational psychology research on teaching students with learning difficulties.* Melbourne: Australian Council for Educational Research.

Emmett, S. (2007). *Two literacy projects – A most insightful association.* Darwin: Charles Darwin University. Retrieved February 28, 2008 from: http://www.aare.edu.au/07pap/emm07195.pdf

Englert, C. S., & Mariage, T. V. (1991). Making students partners in the comprehension process: Organizing the reading 'POSSE'. *Learning Disability Quarterly, 14, 2,* 123–138.

Escribano, C. L. (2007). Evaluation of the double-deficit hypothesis subtype classification of readers of Spanish. *Journal of Learning Disabilities, 40, 4,* 319–330.

Exley, B. (2007). Australian children catch the bug: Motivating young children to engage in reading. *Young Children, 62, 6,* 36–40.

Finn, C. E. (2000). Foreword. In L. Moats, *Whole language lives on: The illusion of 'balanced' reading instruction.* Washington, DC: Thomas Fordham Foundation.

Fisher, B., Bruce, M., & Greive, C. (2007). Look-Say-Cover-Write-Check and Old Way/New Way Mediational Learning: A comparison of the effectiveness of two tutoring programs for children with persistent spelling difficulties. *Special Education Perspectives, 16, 1,* 19–38.

Flynn, N. (2007). What do effective teachers of literacy do? Subject knowledge and pedagogical choices in literacy. *Literacy, 41, 3*, 137–146.

Fountas, I. C., & Pinnell, G. S. (1996). *Guided reading.* Portsmouth, NH: Heinemann.

Fountas, I. C., & Pinnell, G. S. (2001). *Guiding readers and writers in Grades 3–6.* Portsmouth, NH: Heinemann.

Fountas, I. C., & Pinnell, G. S. (2006). *Leveled books (K–8): Matching texts to readers for effective teaching.* Portsmouth, NH: Heinemann.

Freebody, P. (1992). A socio-cultural approach: Resourcing four roles as a literacy learner. In A. Watson, & A. Badenhop (Eds.), *Prevention of reading failure.* Sydney: Ashton Scholastic.

Fresch, M. J. (2007). Teachers' concerns about spelling instruction: A national survey. *Reading Psychology, 28, 4*, 301–330.

Fuchs, D., Fuchs, L. S., Mathes, P. G., & Simmons, D. C. (1997). Peer-assisted learning strategies: Making classrooms more responsive to diversity. *American Educational Research Journal, 34, 1*, 174–206.

Gee, J. (1996). *Social linguistics and literacies: Ideology in discourses* (2nd ed.). London: Taylor & Francis.

German, D. J., & Newman, R. S. (2007). Oral reading skills of children with oral language (word finding) difficulties. *Reading Psychology, 28, 5*, 397–442.

Gersten, R., Fuchs, L. S., Williams, J. P., & Baker, S. (2001). Teaching reading comprehension strategies to students with learning disabilities: A review of research. *Review of Educational Research, 71, 2*, 279–320.

Goldsworthy, C. L. (2001). *Sourcebook of phonological awareness activities.* San Diego, CA: Singular Publishing.

Gough, P. B., & Tunmer, W. E. (1986). Decoding, reading and reading disability. *Remedial and Special Education, 7*, 6–10.

Graham, L., & Bellert, A. (2005). Reading comprehension difficulties experienced by students with learning disabilities. *Australian Journal of Learning Disabilities, 10, 2*, 71–78.

Graham, L., Bellert, A., Thomas, J., & Pegg, J. (2007). Quick-Smart: A basic academic skills intervention for middle school students with learning difficulties. *Journal of Learning Disabilities, 40, 5*, 410–419.

Graham, L., & Wong, B. Y. L. (1993). Comparing two modes of teaching a question-answering strategy for enhancing reading comprehension: Didactic and self-instructional training. *Journal of Learning Disabilities, 26, 4*, 270–279.

Graham, S. (2000). Should the natural learning approach replace spelling instruction? *Journal of Educational Psychology, 92, 2*, 235–247.

Graham, S., & Harris, K. R. (1994). Implications of constructivism for teaching writing to students with special needs. *Journal of Special Education, 28, 3*, 275–289.

Graham, S., & Harris, K. R. (2003). Literacy: Writing. In L. Nandel (Ed.) *Encyclopedia of cognitive science* (vol. 2. pp. 939–945). London: Nature Publishing Group.

Graham, S., & Harris, K. R. (2005). Improving the writing performance of young struggling writers. *Journal of Special Education, 39, 1,* 19–33.

Graham, S., Harris, K. R., & Fink, B. (2000). Is handwriting causally related to learning to write? Treatment of handwriting problems in beginning writers. *Journal of Educational Psychology, 92, 4,* 620–633.

Graham, S., Harris, K. R., Fink-Chorzempa, B., Moran, S., & Saddler, B. (2008). How do primary grade teachers teach handwriting? *Reading and Writing: An Interdisciplinary Journal, 21,* 49–69.

Graham, S., & Perin, D. (2007a). What we know and what we still need to know: Teaching adolescents to write. *Scientific Studies of Reading, 11, 4,* 313–335.

Graham, S., & Perin, D. (2007b). *Writing next: Effective strategies to improve the writing of adolescents in middle and high schools.* Washington, DC: Alliance for Excellence in Education. Retrieved March 31, 2008 from: http://www.carnegie.org/literacy/pdf/writingnext.pdf

Graves, D. H. (1983). *Writing: Teachers and children at work.* Exeter, NH: Heinemann.

Gray, B., & Cowey, W. (2005). *Key elements of scaffolding literacy: Pedagogy and teacher support.* Canberra: Schools and Community Centre, University of Canberra.

Gunning, T.G. (2000). *Building words: A resource manual for teaching word analysis and spelling strategies.* Boston: Allyn & Bacon.

Hall, K., & Harding, A. (2003). A systematic review of effective literacy teaching in the 4 to 14 age range of mainstream schooling. In *Research Evidence in Education Library.* London: EPPI-Centre, Social Sciences Research Unit, University of London.

Hansen, S. (2002). 'Writing Sux!' Boys and writing: What's the problem? *SET Research Information for Teachers, 1,* 38–43.

Harris, K. R., Graham, S., & Mason, L. (2002). POW plus TREE equals powerful opinion essays. *Teaching Exceptional Children, 34, 5,* 74–77.

Hasbrouck, J., & Tindal, G. A. (2006). Oral reading fluency norms: A valuable assessment tool for reading teachers. *The Reading Teacher, 59, 7,* 636–44.

Hay, I., Elias, G., & Booker, G. (2005). Students with learning difficulties in relation to literacy and numeracy. *Schooling Issues Digest 2005/1.* Canberra: Department of Education, Science and Training. Retrieved March 31, 2008 from: http://www.dest.gov.au/sectors/school_education/publications_resources/schooling_issues_digest/schooling_issues_digest_learning_difficulties.htm

Hay, I., & Fielding-Barnsley, R. (2006). Enhancing the early literacy development of children at risk for reading difficulties. *Australian Journal of Learning Disabilities, 11, 3,* 117–124.

Heath, S., Claessen, M., Fletcher, J., Leitao, S., & Hogben, J. (2006). Rapid automatized naming (RAN): A separate influence on literacy outcomes. *Learning Difficulties Australia Bulletin, 38, 1*, 12–14.

Heilman, A. W. (2006). *Phonics in proper perspective* (10th ed.). Upper Saddle River, NJ: Merrill-Prentice Hall.

Heinsch, B. (2001). Case studies using 'Co:Writer' and 'Write:OutLoud'. *Australian Journal of Learning Disabilities, 6, 3*, 24–30.

Hempenstall, K. (2005). Literacy for all is a noble goal: The hurdle of teacher mistraining. *Learning Difficulties Australia Bulletin, 37, 3*, 11–15.

Hempenstall, K. (2006). Balanced golf instruction. *Learning Difficulties Australia Bulletin, 38, 3*, 8–9.

Hess, M., & Wheldall, K. (1999). Strategies for improving the written expression of primary children with poor writing skills. *Australian Journal of Learning Disabilities 4, 4*, 14–20.

Hetzroni, O. E., & Shrieber, B. (2004). Word processing as an assistive technology tool for enhancing academic outcomes of students with writing disabilities in the general classroom. *Journal of Learning Disabilities, 37, 2*, 143–54.

Hoover, W. A., & Gough, P. B. (1990). The simple view of reading. *Reading and Writing, 2*, 127–160.

Horner, S. L., & O'Connor, E. A. (2007). Helping beginning and struggling readers to develop self-regulated strategies: A Reading Recovery example. *Reading and Writing Quarterly, 23*, 97–109.

House of Commons Education and Skills Committee (UK). (2005). *Teaching Children to Read*, London: HMSO.

Hummel, S. (2000). Developing comprehension skills of secondary students with specific learning difficulties. *Australian Journal of Learning Difficulties, 5, 4*, 22–27.

Hurry, J., & Sylva, K. (2007). Long-term outcomes of early reading intervention. *Journal of Research in Reading, 30, 3*, 227–248.

IRA/NAEYC (International Reading Association/National Association for the Education of Young Children). (1998). *Learning to read and write: Developmentally appropriate practices for young children.* Joint statement issued by IRA-NAEYC. Washington, DC: NAEYC. Retrieved February 21, 2008 from: http://www. naeyc.org/about/positions/psread0.asp

Isaacson, S. (2004). Instruction that helps students meet state standards in writing. *Exceptionality, 12, 1*, 39–54.

Jenkins, J., & O'Connor, R. (2001). *Early identification and intervention for young children with reading/learning disabilities.* ERIC document: ED 458757.

Johnston, F. (2001). Exploring classroom teachers' spelling practices and beliefs. *Reading Research and Instruction, 40*, 143–156.

Johnston, R. S., & Morrison, M. (2007). Toward a resolution of inconsistencies in the phonological deficit theory of reading disorders. *Journal of Learning Disabilities, 40, 1*, 66–79.

Johnston, R., & Watson, J. (2005). A seven year study of the effects of synthetic phonics teaching on reading and spelling attainment. *Insight 17.* Edinburgh: Scottish Executive Education Department.

Jongejan, W., Verhoeven, L., & Siegel, L. S. (2007). Predictors of reading and spelling abilities in first- and second-language learners. *Journal of Educational Psychology, 99, 4*, 835–851.

Kairaluoma, L., Ahonen, T., Aro, M., & Holopainen, L. (2007). Boosting reading fluency: An intervention case study at sub-word level. *Scandinavian Journal of Educational Research, 51, 3*, 253–274.

Kelly, G. (2006). A check on Look, Cover, Write, Check. *Learning Difficulties Australia Bulletin, 38, 1*, 6–7.

Kemple, J., Corrin, W., Nelson, E., Salinger, T., Herrmann, S., & Drummond, K. (2008). *The Enhanced Reading Opportunities study: Early impact and implementation findings.* Washington, DC: Institute of Education Sciences and US Department of Education.

Kennedy, G. (2000). Voiced software packages for literacy. *Australian Journal of Learning Disabilities, 5, 4*, 31–32.

Kirkbride, S., & Wright, B. C. (2002). The role of analogy use in improving early spelling performance. *Educational and Child Psychology, 19, 4*, 91–102.

Klinger, J. K., Vaughn, S., & Boardman, A. (2007). *Teaching reading comprehension to students with learning difficulties.* New York: Guilford Press.

Kourea, L., Cartledge, G., & Musti-Rao, S. (2007). Improving the reading skills of urban elementary students through total class peer tutoring. *Remedial and Special Education, 28, 2*, 95–107.

Lam, B. F. Y., & Westwood, P. (2006). Spelling and ESL learners: A strategy training approach. *Special Education Perspectives, 15, 1*, 12–24.

Le Bigot, L., & Rouet, J. F. (2007). The impact of presentation format, task assignment and prior knowledge on students' comprehension of multiple online documents. *Journal of Literacy Research, 39, 4*, 445–470.

LeVasseu, V. M., Macaruso, P., & Shankweiler, D. (2008). Promoting gains in reading fluency: A comparison of three approaches. *Reading and Writing: An Interdisciplinary Journal, 21, 3*, 177–297.

Lietz, P. (1996). Learning and writing difficulties at the tertiary level: Their impact on first year results. *Studies in Educational Evaluation, 22, 1*, 41–57.

Lin, S. J. C., Monroe, B. W., & Troia, G. A. (2007). Development of writing knowledge in grades 2–8: A comparison of typically developing writers and their struggling peers. *Reading and Writing Quarterly, 23, 3*, 207–230.

Lindstrom, J. H. (2007). Determining appropriate accommodations for post-secondary students with reading and written expression disorders. *Learning Disabilities Research and Practice, 22, 4*, 229–236.

Lloyd, S., & Wernham, S. (1995). *Jolly Phonics Workbooks.* Chigwell, Essex: Jolly Learning.

Louden, W., Rohl, M., Barratt-Pugh, C., Brown, C., Cairney, T., Elderfield, J., House, H., Meiers, M., Rivalland, J., & Rowe, K. (2005). 'In Teachers' Hands': Effective literacy teaching practices in the early years of schooling. *Australian Journal of Language and Literacy, 28, 3*, 181–253.

Lovett, M. W., Lacerenza, L., Borden, S. L., Frijters, J. C., Steinbach, K. A., & De Palma, M. (2000). Components of effective remediation for developmental reading disabilities: Combining phonological and strategy-based instruction to improve outcomes. *Journal of Educational Psychology, 92*, 263–283.

Luke, A., & Carrington, V. (2002). Globalisation, literacy, curriculum practice. In G. Brooks, R. Fisher, & M. Lewis (Eds.), *Language and Literacy in action* (pp. 231–250). London: Routledge-Falmer.

Lyndon, H. (1989). I did it my way: An introduction to Old Way–New Way. *Australasian Journal of Special Education 13*, 32–7.

MacArthur, C. A. (2000). New tools for writing: Assistive technology for students with writing difficulties. *Topics in Language Disorders, 20, 4*, 85–100.

Macmillan, B. (2003). *Synthetic phonics: The scientific research evidence.* Online document retrieved March 18, 2008 from: http://www.jollylearning.co.uk/research2.htm

Magliano, J. P., Trabasso, T., & Graesser, A. C. (1999). Strategic processing during comprehension. *Journal of Educational Psychology, 91, 4*, 615–629.

Mandlebaum, L. H., Hodges, D., & Messenheimer, T. (2007). Get students to read it again. *Intervention in School and Clinic, 42, 5*, 295–299.

Masters, G., & Forster, M. (1997a) *Literacy standards in Australia.* Canberra: Commonwealth of Australia.

Masters, G., & Forster, M. (1997b). *Mapping literacy achievement results of the 1996 National School English Literacy Survey.* Canberra: Commonwealth Department of Education, Employment, Training and Youth Affairs.

McCardle, P., Scarborough, H. S., & Catts, H. W. (2002). Predicting, explaining and preventing children's reading difficulties. *The Quarterly Bulletin of the Remedial and Support Teachers' Association of Queensland*, December Issue 2002, 5–17.

MCEETYA (Ministerial Council on Education, Employment, Training and Youth Affairs). (2008). *National Report on Schooling in Australia: National benchmark results in reading, writing and numeracy Years 3, 5 and 7.* Canberra: MCEETYA.

McKown, B. A., & Barnett, C. L. (2007). Improving reading comprehension through higher-order thinking skills. MA degree research project: Saint Xavier University, Chicago, IL. Retrieved February 18, 2008 from: http://www.eric.ed.gov/ERICDocs/data/ericdocs2sql/content_storage_01/0000019b/80/28/09/00.pdf

McMaster, K. L., Fuchs, D., & Fuchs, L. S. (2006). Research on peer-assisted learning strategies: The promise and the limitations of peer-mediated instruction. *Reading & Writing Quarterly, 22, 1,* 5–25.

McQuillan, J. (1998). *The literacy crisis: False claims, real solutions.* Portsmouth, NH: Heinemann.

Medwell, J., & Wray, D. (2007). Handwriting: What do we know and what do we need to know? *Literacy, 41, 1,* 10–15.

Medwell, J., & Wray, D. (2008). Handwriting: A forgotten language skill? *Language and Education, 22, 1,* 34–47.

Meiers, M., Khoo, S. T., Rowe, K., Stephanou, A., Anderson, P., & Nolan, K. (2006). *Growth in literacy and numeracy in the first 3 years of school.* Melbourne: Australian Council for Educational Research.

Mesmer, H. A. E., & Griffith, P. L. (2006). Everybody's selling it – but just what is explicit, systematic phonics instruction? *Reading Teacher 59, 4,* 366–76.

Ministry of Education (New Zealand). (2007). *Literacy Professional Development Project: Identifying effective teaching and professional development practices for enhancing student learning.* Retrieved March 11, 2008 from: http://www.educationcounts.govt.nz/publications/literacy

Moats, L. (1995). *Spelling: Development, disability and instruction.* Baltimore: York Press.

Moats, L. (1999). *Reading IS rocket science: What expert teachers of reading should know and be able to do.* Washington, DC: American Federation of Teachers. Retrieved February 22, 2008 from: http://www.aft.org/pubs-reports/downloads/teachers/rocketsci.pdf

Moats, L. (2000). *Whole language lives on: The illusion of 'balanced' reading instruction.* Washington, DC: Thomas Fordham Foundation.

Moats, L. (2007). *Whole language high jinks: How to tell when 'scientifically-based reading instruction' isn't.* Washington, DC: Thomas Fordham Institute.

Myers, L., & Botting, N. (2008). Literacy in the mainstream inner-city school: Its relationship to spoken language. *Child Language Teaching and Therapy, 24, 1,* 95–114.

NALP (National Accelerated Literacy Program). (2007). *Methodology.* Retrieved February 28, 2008 from: http://www.nalp.edu.au/spelling.html

National Commission on Writing. (2003). *The neglected 'R': The need for a writing revolution.* New York. The College Board.

National Commission on Writing. (2006). *Writing and school reform.* New York: The College Board.

National Council on Teacher Quality. (2006). *What education schools aren't teaching about reading and what elementary teachers aren't learning.* Washington, DC: NCTQ.

National Reading Panel (US). (2000). *Teaching children to read: An evidence-based assessment of the scientific research literature on reading and its implications for reading instruction.* Washington, DC: National Institute of Child Health and Human Development.

Neill, M. (2005). Total recall. *Special Children, 164,* 22–25.

Neufeld, P. (2006). Comprehension instruction in content area classes. *Reading Teacher 59, 4,* 302–12.

Nicholson, T. (1998). Teaching reading: The flashcard strikes back. *Reading Teacher, 52, 2,* 188–192.

Nicholson, T. (2006). How to avoid reading failure: teach phonemic awareness. In A. McKeough, J. L. Lupart, L. M. Phillips, & V. Timmons (Eds.), *Understanding literacy development: A global view.* Mahwah, NJ: Erlbaum.

Oakley, G. (2002). Using CD-ROM 'Electronic talking books' to help children with mild reading difficulties improve their reading fluency. *Australian Journal of Learning Disabilities, 7, 4,* 20–27.

O'Brien, D., Beach, R., & Scharber, C. (2007). Struggling middle schoolers: Engagement and literate competence in a reading, writing intervention class. *Reading Psychology, 28,1,* 51–73.

Oczkus, L. D. (2007). *Guided writing: Practical lessons, powerful results.* Portsmouth, NH: Heinemann.

OECD (Organisation for Economic Cooperation and Development). (2007) *Education at a glance 2007.* Paris: OECD.

OECD (Organisation for Economic Cooperation and Development). (2008). *Teaching, learning and assessment for adults: Improving foundation skills.* Paris: OECD.

Ogle, D. (1986). K-W-L: A teaching model that develops active reading of expository text. *The Reading Teacher, 39,* 564–570.

Pearce, S., Wheldall, K., & Madelaine, A. (2006). Multilit book levels: Towards a new system for leveling texts. *Special Education Perspectives, 15, 1,* 38–56.

Perin, D. (2006). Can community colleges protect both access and standards? The problem of remediation. *Teachers College Record, 108, 3,* 339–373.

Peters, M. L. (1974). Teacher variables in spelling. In B. Wade & K. Wedell (Eds.), *Spelling: Task and learner.* Birmingham: University of Birmingham Press.

Phillips, D. (2004). Writing with a word processor. *SET: Research Information for Teachers, 3/2004* (pp. 6–8). Wellington: New Zealand Council for Educational Research.

Pikulski, J. J. (1997). *A balanced approach to literacy.* Retrieved February 21, 2008 from: http://www.eduplace.com/rdg/res/teach/index.html

Polkinghorne, J. (2004). Electronic literacy: Part 1 and Part 2. *Australian Journal of Learning Disabilities, 9, 2,* 24–27.

Pollington, M. F., Wilcox, B., & Morrison, T. G. (2001). Self-perception in writing: The effects of writing workshop and traditional instruction on intermediate grade students. *Reading Psychology, 22,* 249–65.

Pressley, M. (2006). *Reading instruction that works: The case for balanced teaching* (3rd ed.). New York: Guilford.

Pressley, M., & Hilden, K. (2006). Teaching reading comprehension. In A. McKeough, L. M. Phillips, V. Timmons, & J. L. Lupart (Eds.), *Understanding literacy development: A global view.* Mahwah, NJ: Erlbaum.

Prior, M. (1996). *Understanding specific learning difficulties.* Hove: Psychology Press.

Rapp, D. N., van den Broek, P., McMaster, K. L., Kendeou, P., & Espin, C.A. (2007). Higher-order comprehension processes in struggling readers: A perspective for research and intervention. *Scientific Studies of Reading, 11, 4,* 289–312.

Raven, I. (2003). The end of the reading wars? *Journal of the Simplified Spelling Society, 32, 1,* 4–8. Retrieved February 21, 2008 from: http://www.spellingsociety.org/journals/j32/wars.php

Rayner, K. (1997). Understanding eye movements in reading. *Scientific Studies of Reading, 1, 4,* 317–339.

Ricketts, J., Bishop, D. V. M., & Nation, K. (2008). Investigating orthographic and semantic aspects of word learning in poor comprehenders. *Journal of Research in Reading, 31, 1,* 117–135.

Rief, L. (2006). What's right with writing. *Voices from the Middle, 13, 4,* 32–39.

Robinson, G. (2001). Problems in literacy and numeracy. In P. Foreman (Ed.), *Integration and inclusion in action* (2nd ed.)(pp. 169–229). Melbourne: Nelson-Thomson.

Romeo, L. (2008). Informal writing assessment linked to instruction: A continuous process for teachers, students and parents. *Reading and Writing Quarterly, 24, 1,* 25–51.

Rose, J. (2006). *Independent review of the teaching of early reading: Final report.* London: Department for Education and Skills.

Rowe, K. (2006). Teaching reading: Findings from the National Inquiry. *ACER Research Development, 15,* 1–4. Retrieved March 30, from: http://www.acer.edu.au/resdev/15_TeachingReading.html

Sabbatino, E. (2004). Students with learning disabilities construct meaning through graphic organizers: Strategies for achievement in inclusive classrooms. *Learning Disabilities: A Multidisciplinary Journal, 13, 2,* 69–74.

Saddler, B. (2006). Increasing story writing ability through self-regulated strategy development: Effects on young writers with learning disabilities. *Learning Disability Quarterly, 29, 4,* 291–305.

Saddler, B., & Graham, S. (2007). The relationship between writing knowledge and writing performance among more and less skilled writers. *Reading and Writing Quarterly, 23, 3,* 231–247.

Saddler, B., Moran, S., Graham, S., & Harris, K. R. (2004). Preventing writing difficulties: The effects of planning strategy instruction on the writing performance of struggling writers. *Exceptionality, 12, 1,* 3–17.

Savage, R., & Frederickson, N. (2006). Beyond phonology: What else is needed to describe the problems of below average readers and spellers? *Journal of Learning Disabilities, 39, 5,* 399–413.

Savage, R., Lavers, N., & Pillay, V. (2007). Working memory and reading difficulties: What we know and what we don't know. *Educational Psychology Review, 19, 2,* 185–221.

Sawyer W., & Watson, K. (1997). Literacy issues in Australia. *Teacher Development, 1, 3,* 457–464.

Schilling, S. G., Carlisle, J. F., Scott, S. E., & Zeng, J. (2007). Are fluency measures accurate predictors of reading achievement? *Elementary School Journal, 107, 5,* 429–448.

Schumaker, J. B., & Deshler, D. D. (2003). Can students with LD become competent writers? *Learning Disabilities Quarterly, 26, 2,* 129–141.

Senate Standing Committee on Employment, Workplace Relations and Education. (2007). *Quality of school education.* Retrieved April 5, 2008 from: http://www.aph.gov.au/SENATE/committee/EET_CTTE/completed_inquiries/2004-07/academic_standards/report/index.htm

Sencibaugh, J. M. (2007). Meta-analysis of reading comprehension interventions for students with learning disabilities: Strategies and implications. *Reading Improvement, 44, 1,* 6–22.

Shahar-Yames, D., & Share, D. L. (2008). Spelling as a self-teaching mechanism in orthographic learning. *Journal of Research in Reading, 31, 3,* 22–39.

Silva, C., & Alves-Martins, M. A. (2003). Relations between children's invented spelling and the development of phonological awareness. *Educational Psychology, 23, 1*, 4–16.

Simmons, D. C., Kameenui, E. F., Harn, B., Coyne, M. D., Stoolmiller, M., Santoro, L. E., Smith, S. B., Beck, C. T., & Kaufman, N. K. (2007). Attributes of effective and efficient kindergarten reading interventions: An examination of instructional time and design specificity. *Journal of Learning Disabilities, 40, 4*, 331–347.

Skylar, A. A., Higgins, K., & Boone, R. (2007). Strategies for adapting WebQuests for students with learning disabilities. *Intervention in School and Clinic, 43, 1*, 20–28.

Slavin, R. E., & Madden, N. A. (2001). *One million children: Success for All.* Thousand Oaks, CA: Corwin Press.

Smith, C. (2001). *A quality evaluation of the Schoolwide Early Language and Literacy (SWELL) program in Maitland-Newcastle Diocesan Catholic schools.* Retrieved March 24, 2008 from: http://mn.catholic.edu.au/projects/evaluation.pdf

Snowball, D. (2005). Directed Reading–Thinking Activity. From *Teaching comprehension: An interactive professional development course.* New York: Aussie Interactive. Retrieved April 4, 2008 from: http://www.curriculum.org/secretariat/files/Oct25reading.pdf

South Australian Government. (2007). *South Australia's Action Plan for literacy and numeracy.* Retrieved February 28, 2008 from: http://www.premcab.sa.gov.au/pdf/coag/coag_ap_literacy.pdf

Spear-Swerling, L. (2007). The research–practice divide in beginning reading. *Theory to Practice, 46, 4*, 301–308.

Stern, S. (2005). A negative assessment: An education revolution that never was. *Education Next, 5, 4*, (n.p.).

Storry, K. (2007). What is working in good schools in remote indigenous communities? *Issue Analysis, 86*, 1–19.

Stotz, K. E., Itoi, M., Konrad, M., & Alber-Morgan, S. (2008). Effects of self-graphing on written expression of fourth grade students with high-incidence disabilities. *Journal of Behavioral Education, 17, 2*, 172–186.

Sturm, J., & Koppenhaver, D. A. (2000). Supporting writing development in adolescents with developmental disabilities. *Topics in Language Disorders, 20, 2*, 73–92.

Sumbler, K., & Willows, D. (1996). *Phonological awareness and alphabetic coding instruction within balanced senior kindergartens.* Paper presented at the National Reading Conference, Charleston, SC, December 1996. Cited in Macmillan (2003).

Swanson, H. L. (2000). What instruction works for students with learning disabilities? In R. Gersten, E. Schiller, & S. Vaughn (Eds.), *Contemporary special education research* (pp. 1–30). Mahwah, NJ: Erlbaum.

Swanson, H. L., & Jerman, O. (2007). The influences of working memory on reading growth in subgroups of children with reading disabilities. *Journal of Experimental Child Psychology, 96, 4,* 249–283.

Tan, K. H., Wheldall, K., Madelaine, A., & Lee, L.W. (2007). A review of the simple view of reading: Decoding and linguistic comprehension skills of low-progress readers. *Australian Journal of Learning Disabilities, 12, 1,* 19–30.

Teale, W. H., Paciga, K. A., & Hoffman, J. L. (2008). Beginning reading instruction in urban schools: The curriculum gap ensures a continuing achievement gap. *Reading Teacher, 61, 4,* 344–348.

Templeton, S. (2003). The spelling–meaning connection. *Voices from the Middle, 10, 3,* 56–57.

Therrien, W. J., Gormley, S., & Kubina, R. M. (2006). Boosting fluency and comprehension to improve reading achievement. *Teaching Exceptional Children, 38, 3,* 22–25.

Thomas, D. G., Reeves, C., Kazelskis, R., York, K., Boling, C., Newell, K., & Wang, Y. (2008). Reading comprehension: Effects of individualised, integrated language arts as a reading approach with struggling readers. *Reading Psychology, 29, 1,* 86–115.

Thomson, M. (1995). Evaluating teaching programs for children with specific learning difficulties. *Australian Journal of Remedial Education, 27, 1,* 20–27.

Thomson, M. B., & Snow, P. C. (2002). The written expression of children with reading disabilities: A comparison of written and dictated narratives. *Australian Journal of Learning Disabilities, 7–4,* 13–19.

Tompkins, G. E. (2006). *Literacy for 21st century: A balanced approach* (4th ed.). Upper Saddle River, NJ: Pearson-Merrill-Prentice Hall.

Topping, K., & Ferguson, N. (2005). Effective literacy teaching behaviours. *Journal of Research in Reading, 28, 2,* 125–143.

Torgesen, J. K. (2000). Individual differences in response to early intervention in reading: The lingering problem of treatment resisters. *Learning Disabilities Research and Practice, 15, 1,* 55–64.

Torgesen, J. (2007). *A principal's guide to intensive reading intervention for struggling readers in Reading First schools.* Florida Centre for Reading Research. ERIC document ED498776.

Tse, S. K., Lam, J. W., Lam, R. H. Y., Loh, E. K. Y., & Westwood, P. (2007). Pedagogical correlates of reading achievement in English and Chinese medium. *L1-Educational Studies in Language and Literacy, 7, 2,* 71–91.

Tunmer, W. E., Chapman, J. W., Greaney, K. T., & Prochnow, J. E. (2002). The contribution of educational psychology to intervention research and practice. *International Journal of Disability, Development and Education 49, 1,* 11–29.

UKLA/ PNS (United Kingdom Literacy Association/ Primary National Strategy). (2004). *Raising boys' achievements in writing.* Royston, Hertfordshire: UKLA.

Vanderburg, R. M. (2006). Reviewing research on teaching writing based on Vygotsky's theories: What we can learn. *Reading and Writing Quarterly, 22,* 375–393.

Vukovic, R. K., & Siegel, L. S. (2006). The double-deficit hypothesis: A comprehensive analysis of the evidence. *Journal of Learning Disabilities, 39, 1,* 25–47.

Walczyk, J. J., & Griffith-Ross, D. A. (2007). How important is reading skill fluency for comprehension? *Reading Teacher, 60, 6,* 560–564.

Weekes, B. S., Hamilton, C., Oakhill, J. V., & Holliday, R. E. (2008). False recollection in children with reading comprehension difficulties. *Cognition, 106, 1,* 222–233.

Weeks, S., Brooks, P., & Everatt, J. (2002). Differences in learning to spell: Relationships between cognitive profiles and learning responses to teaching methods. *Educational and Child Psychology, 19, 4,* 47–62.

Welna, L. D. (1999). Balance and sacred cows: A reply to Reutzel. *Reading Teacher, 53, 2,* 94–95.

Westerveld, M. F., & Gillon, G. T. (2008). Oral narrative intervention for children with mixed reading disability. *Child Language Teaching and Therapy, 24, 1,* 31–54.

Westwood. P. S. (2004). Affective components of difficulty in learning: Why prevention is better than attempted cure. In B. A. Knight & W. Scott (Eds.), *Learning difficulties: Multiple perspectives.* Frenchs Forest, NSW: Pearson Education Australia.

Westwood, P. S. (2007). *Commonsense methods for children with special educational needs* (5th ed.). Abingdon: Routledge.

Westwood, P. S. (2008). *What teachers need to know about teaching methods.* Melbourne: Australian Council for Educational Research.

Wheldall, K. (2006). Whole language being abandoned worldwide. *Learning Difficulties Australia Bulletin, 38, 4,* 3.

Wheldall, K., & Beaman, R. (2007). *Multilit tutor program (revised).* Sydney: Macquarie University.

Whiteley, H. E., Smith, C. D., & Connors, L. (2007). Young children at risk of literacy difficulties: Factors predicting recovery from risk following phonologically based intervention, *Journal of Research in Reading, 30, 3,* 249–269.

Williams, C., & Phillips-Birdsong, C. (2006). Word study instruction and second grade children's independent writing. *Journal of Literacy Research, 38, 4,* 427–465.

Williams, J. P. (2005). Instruction in reading comprehension for primary-grade students: A focus on text structure. *Journal of Special Education, 39, 1,* 6–18.

Willows, D. (2002). The balanced and flexible literacy diet. *The School Administrator* (online). Retrieved June 15, 2008 from: http://www.aasa.org/publications/ saarticledetail.cfm?ItemNumber=2726

Wilson, K. M., & Trainin, G. (2007). First-grade students' motivation and achievement for reading, writing and spelling. *Reading Psychology, 28, 3,* 257–282.

Wilson, R. M. (2003). *Teaching reading: A history.* Retrieved March 12, 2008 from: http://www.zona-pellucida.com/wilson10.html

Wise, J. C., Sevcik, R. A., Morris, R. D., Lovett, M. W., & Wolf, M. (2007a). The relationship among receptive and expressive vocabulary, listening comprehension, pre-reading skills, word identification, skills and reading comprehension by children with reading disabilities. *Journal of Speech, Language and Hearing Research, 50,* 1093–1109.

Wise, J. C., Sevcik, R. A., Morris, R. D., Lovett, M. W., & Wolf, M. (2007b). The growth of phonological awareness by children with reading disabilities: A result of semantic knowledge or knowledge of grapheme-phoneme correspondences? *Scientific Studies of Reading, 11, 2,* 151–164.

Wojasinski, A. M., & Smith, D. M. (2002). *What writing strategy – process, free, or informal – is the most effective for students with learning disabilities?* A paper presented at the Annual Special Education Action Research Conference, South Bend, IN: April 27, 2002. ERIC document ED 466080.

Wolf, M., & Bowers, P. G. (1999). The double-deficit hypothesis for developmental dyslexia. *Journal of Educational Psychology, 91,* 415–438.

Woolley, G. (2007). A comprehension intervention for children with reading comprehension difficulties. *Australian Journal of Learning Disabilities, 12, 1,* 43–50.

Worthy, J., Broaddus, K., & Ivey, G. (2001). *Pathways to independence: Reading, writing and learning in Grades 3–8.* New York: Guilford Press.

Wren, S. (n.d.). What does a balanced literacy approach mean? Online document retrieved February 21, 2008 from: http://www.sedl.org/reading/topics/ balanced.html

Wren, S. (2003). The simple view of reading: R = D × C. Online discussion document retrieved March 15, 2008 from: http://www.balancedreading.com/ simple.html

Xue, Y., & Meisels, S. J. (2004). Early literacy instruction and learning in kindergarten: Evidence from the early childhood longitudinal study –

kindergarten class 1998–1999. *American Educational Research Journal, 41, 1,* 191–229.

Ziolkowska, R. (2007). Early intervention for students with reading and writing difficulties. *Reading Improvement, 44, 2,* 76–86.

Index

Main entries in **bold**